The Other Walk

The Other Walk

Essays

SVEN BIRKERTS

Graywolf Press

Some pieces appeared in slightly different form in *Conjunctions,* conjunctions.com, *AGNI,* www.bu.edu/agni, the *Threepenny Review, A Public Space, Ecotone, Water-Stone Review,* the *Oxford American, Unsaid, Almost Island, Pushcart Prize XXXIV,* and *Corridors.*

This publication is made possible by funding provided in part by a grant from the Minnesota State Arts Board, through an appropriation by the Minnesota State Legislature, a grant from the National Endowment for the Arts, and private funders. Significant support has also been provided by Target; the McKnight Foundation; and other generous contributions from foundations, corporations, and individuals. To these organizations and individuals we offer our heartfelt thanks.

Published by Graywolf Press
250 Third Avenue North, Suite 600
Minneapolis, Minnesota 55401

www.graywolfpress.org

Published in the United States of America
Printed in Canada

ISBN 978-1-55597-593-7

2 4 6 8 9 7 5 3 1
First Graywolf Printing, 2011

Library of Congress Control Number: 2011930481

Cover design: Kyle G. Hunter

Cover photo: Lise Metzger/Stone/Getty Images

For my family and for all of you who move like apparitions of memory through these pages

Contents

The Other Walk   3

Zvirbulis   6

Grandfather's Painting   14

Fury   18

Lost Things   20

Schimmelpenninck   24

Head   28

Wink   32

Old Glasses   34

Schoolroom   37

The Friend   40

Plunge   46

"Blue Melody"   47

Barcelona   50

Chessboard   53

Cup   57

Postcard   59

Finding the Level   64

Ladder   68

Tomcat   73

Apple   77

It   79

Lighter   83

Photo: Father-in-Law   86

Stone Shard   89

Brown Loafers   92

Walking with My Friend   95

Photo, Ring   97

Rufus and Lenny   100

In Another City   104

The Finger Writes   106

Archive   108

Papa   111

Reading Oneself   114

The German Poet   116

What Is the Poet?   119

As Above: Saul Bellow   121

What Do *You* Do
   for Work, Daddy?   129

Every Day   132   The Points of Sail   145

Starbucks   134   Walden   160

Coffee   137   The Walk   171

Magda   140

The Other Walk

The Other Walk

This morning, going against all convention, I turned right instead of left and took my circuit—one of my circuits—in reverse. Why hadn't I thought of this before, given that the familiarity of the other loop has become so oppressive, even to one who swears by the zen of familiarity, the main tenet being that if you are bored with what you're seeing, you're not seeing clearly enough, not looking? Still, going against the grain of my usual track, seeing every single thing from the other side, was suddenly welcome. It also helped that it felt like the first real spring day, the birds more liquid in their vowels, and the waft of that elusive something added to the usual air. Habit and repetition. It's not as if I don't know this other walk intimately, too—not as if I haven't taken it hundreds of times over what are now becoming these years of walking. How is it I haven't written more on this topic? It's been a big part of the day's business for years. I don't remember when I started. Easily seven or eight years ago, maybe more. For a long time walking vied with swimming—walking was what I did when I couldn't get myself into a pool or pond in the early morning. Then swimming gradually waned, and this took over. Five, six mornings a week, year-round. And so many phases. The edgy, anxious midlife walks that for so long were my only recourse to sleeplessness. I would wake in the dark all wired up and needing to push against myself, to burn off the gnawing, no choice but to get out. In those days the circuits were vast, miles and miles, all of them covered at a clip, the point being not to see anything but to get into the day in a way I could stand, that was not intolerable. And the walking would eventually bring me around—after the up and down of the neighborhood streets, down along the edge of the playing fields, onto the bike path, which I would follow for a good mile or so, before hooking up with the long road winding back past the Busa farm stand, though it was really only in that last stretch, coming up to Busa, that I would feel my body and breath get into sync. . . .

Psychic news travels. After some months of this solo morning mania, my daughter, Mara, started asking if she could walk with me. She would make me promise to get her up, even though it was still dark outside, even though she had school to get ready for, and she would join me. Morning after morning she would bundle up in her sweatshirt and the two of us would head out. Sometimes I felt sorry for her and we made a modified loop, but other mornings she insisted that we go the distance. And we did. We talked, or not. There were many days when we moved in our separate worlds, I walking ahead, she trailing. She was having anxieties of her own—she was in love and it was unrequited. And then it was requited. But she kept on with our ritual. She would always leave the same little sticky note at the top of the stairs: "Wake me if you walk, Dad." She was very much afraid that I would go without her. I wondered about this, her determination, and only much later did I learn that she was worried about me. She hated to think of me by myself in the early morning, didn't want me to be sad. This went on for many seasons. It never stopped abruptly, but there were more and more mornings when it was hard for her to get up, when I would touch her shoulder and assure her that I was fine, that she could join me the next day. And sometimes she did. Now more time has passed. Mara is away at college, and I still go out, almost every morning. But the loops are smaller. I don't go the great distances anymore, and I don't go to calm myself. Now I go from habit, and to start the day. If I didn't look at things so much before, now I do. I start down the street and let my gaze swing this way and that, taking in the sky, the outlines of branches, the crazing of the pavement. I feel myself stretching, working my way into a rhythm. Around the local bends and onto the path that goes around the Reed's Brook Park Reservation, which is not much of a reservation, but has tall hardy grasses on the left, which fill me with a boyhood sense of the Midwest, and the swampy area on the other side, high with bamboo weeds, and in the spring and summer full of red-winged blackbirds. Then I round the bend to the left where the water stretches out—suspect, contaminated, but still taking the light, and home to ducks and geese and, at certain times, a single heron. Last year that heron became my goal: as soon as I followed the bend I would begin my careful perusing of the reedy indentations, looking for the distinctive silhouette, that long beak protruding at a forty-five-degree angle, the exciting stillness that gathers around creatures that are poised for the hunt. When people ask about these walks I say that I use them to set up the writing day, to start my thinking. And it's true. Usually by the time I get back I have some basic sequences worked out; I think about projects. I'll get hooked on some thought, and I'll go over it repeatedly, as if inscribing it into my muscles, but also testing its basic hardiness against the rhythms of walking. The wispier thoughts tend to dissolve and float away; the more durable ones settle in and then start thudding in my head. This morning—did I think this morning? Or did I just try to get a sense of the day? I was out just a short while back, but I can't remember, and maybe that's another thing about these hours: that they are unto themselves, not an aspect of the day, but a prelude to it. I planned, I thought, and I honestly don't think I can recover much of either plans or thoughts. All I get right now, thinking back, is an impression I had coming down the hill, heading toward the other gate, of clouds looking soft and mussed up around the edges, red gray. And yes, I did think, right then, that spring does have its own special character, unlike any other time, and that part of what happens in spring is remembering we have it in us to surprise ourselves—things do come fresh again.

Zvirbulis

For the first twenty years of my life I believed that we were the only Birkertses in the world, our little family of four (only much later, five)—no relatives, no outliers, just us. But then one day when I was already on my own, home on a visit, my father passed a photograph across the table to me. It was a casual gesture, offered in the spirit of "here, look what we saw." He and my mother were just back from a trip to Europe. They had been in Germany, in Stuttgart, where my father went to school after the war. The photo showed a storefront: simple, no frills, with the lettered sign BIRKERTS prominently over the door. It took me a moment to get what I was looking at, but as soon as I did I registered a nervous tremor in my deepest core. The idea that there were other people moving through the world with my name, signing documents, maybe answering classroom roll calls, unsettled me. So much for my longstanding myth of singularity. Not that I *needed* to think of myself as unique, one of a kind. But I always had. There was just the little group of us all that time. Identity crystallizes subtly around just such assumptions. But no more. What did the people look like? What did they sell there? Did locals say things like, "If you go past Birkerts's . . ." I thought about this for a time, and then I forgot, and the old assumptions more or less settled back into place.

Birkerts is a German name, but both sides of my family are Latvian all the way back. For a good part of its history, though, and presumably at the time of what I used to imagine was the great conferring of names, Latvia was ruled by German land barons, and some of us, mainly those who served, were tagged by the local powers that be. Who knows how it worked, why this name or that? Birkerts. I was always told that it meant "of the birch," and from childhood on I've considered that stippled white-barked tree one of my two totems. When I see birches, anywhere, at any time—it's automatic now—I feel a reaffirming sort of vibration.

My other totem is the sparrow. This one has to do with Latvians and their ancient pagan culture, and the animistic tendency to assign people surnames according to creaturely associations. A great many Latvians carry these original identifiers, surnames like Balodis (pigeon) or Vilks (wolf) or—on my mother's side of the family—Zvirbulis, meaning "sparrow." My mother was Sylvia Zvirbulis, and to look at her, or at any photograph of my grandfather, is to understand the logic of bestowal. Even now, when he is in the mood to prod her a bit, my father will address her as *spitze Nase,* meaning "sharp nose" or "pointy nose." To which she responds as she has for years—with a funny little sparrowish movement, shaking her head and making a few quick beaky stabs at the air in front of her.

Literal physical association is one thing, fairly quickly exhausted as a quirk, but I wonder about the deeper business. For I don't believe that such coinages were undertaken in a spirit of pure whimsy—these are *family names* after all. Nor do I think any attribution would have stuck if there hadn't been some genuine felt congruence—just like I don't believe that the words of any language were created by simple fiat. I want it to be that they survived and entered the repertoire because of their essential poetic fitness. Emerson wrote that every word is at root a poem, by which he meant an incarnation of some deeply felt reality into a sound. Language mysticism, yes—but I do subscribe. And then, subscribed, I have to wonder not only whether there was something beyond a conspicuous pointiness of nose but also—more interesting to me—if the deeper family soul didn't in some subtle way keep faith, align itself, italicize in itself some essential sparrowness.

You would think that if I were so intrigued by this I would have long since done some research on my namesake bird, but I haven't, not a bit. This is evidence of my laziness, to be sure. But it's also part of a larger self-consistency—I don't seek information if it's not in my natural path of action to seek it. I resist researching even the things that interest me— at least if that research requires a deliberated step to the side of whatever I think I'm doing. So I have no real facts about sparrows to conjure with, nothing beyond my ordinary observations, which are, I'll concede, not much. Still, if I had to make a list based just on these incidental noticings I would propose as follows: sparrows are small, brownish and grayish, winged, built for short fluttery flights, watchful, on the lookout for seeds and crumbs, bits of things; they like to perch, singly or with one or two others of their kind; their heartbeats or pulses are on a permanent high-speed setting. Probably they quickly burn whatever they consume.

Outwardly it's obvious that I don't share all that much with the sparrow. I am large, for starters. Brownish and grayish, OK, that fits. But I don't have wings—and generally think of myself as a distance man, a long hauler: long swims, long walks. I do fancy myself as watchful—vigilant—but only in certain respects (about shifts in people's moods, about words, spoken and written or printed), while remaining famously oblivious (*obtuse* is an adjective that gets used) to appearances, niceties, the accepted value of things . . . Crumbs and seeds don't often pique me, but I do enjoy perching, fixing myself in places so that I can watch. For example, I don't mind waiting at airports or bus stations, provided I can set up to slowly survey whatever is around me. This is the opposite of research, a kind of relenting to circumstance that allows for a focus otherwise not available to me. But my perching has to be solo. I don't like to have others, even others of my kind, anywhere near. I'm a solitary creature. And my pulse and heartbeat are not at all on high—quite the reverse. I can only dream of burning off what I consume. I'm hardly like a sparrow in most ways, but I would be lying if I said I didn't feel a sweet, almost secret-seeming bond with the little creatures whenever they cross my path. And they cross my path almost every day.

I see them when I go out walking, which I do every morning, pretty much without exception. Either I go in the direction of town, in which case they are up there on the wires or flustering around in hedges and bushes; or else I follow a track through the little preserve area down the street, where they always find themselves outnumbered and outgunned by the red-winged blackbirds. These flashier birds are a direct circuit back to my Michigan childhood—the swamps that were my stalking grounds—and I can't resist following their flights. In fact, I get so distracted by the sudden flares of bright red that if I want to see my namesakes I have to forcibly redirect my attention. This is not what attention is ultimately about—it's like telling yourself to be impulsive—but it works well enough to give me that flicker of connection.

My picture of Latvia—my postcard—is a place of lakes and fields and birches, another of the idealized figments by which I live. But I got my impression early on and very clearly. Certainly the Latvian land-scape paintings I grew up looking at—including those done by my grandfather—convey that basic essence. I love the world depicted in these paintings with a sentimental force that is stronger than anything I feel from having been there.

Though I've visited Latvia three times in my life, I was always in the city, in Riga; I have spent almost no time in the countryside. If that country-side seems more vivid to me, it's partly from staring at these paintings, but also because my father used to speak so fondly of his summers growing up when he joined the large gangs of young people who were sent to work on the farms. I must have been at a susceptible age when he first told me his stories, for I've taken the feeling of that life all the way in. Never under-estimate the power of a child's fantasies, or, from the parent's side, the im-pact of what is said, and how it is said, the tone of voice. I'm back to the words and the sounds again, the nouns: *upe* (river), *mezhi* (forests), *lauki* (fields) . . . I absorbed these things with my whole listening self. So much so that even now when I say those words, and a small handful of others, I feel something inside the language open up. Remember, every word was once a poem. Maybe this is why my childhood language has a thickness and density that I hardly ever get with English, though my English over-ran my Latvian fifty years ago. The first spell is the strongest.

The last time I traveled to Latvia I went alone. This was before the col-lapse of communism, so my whole experience had a more than slightly nervous glancing-over-the-shoulder feeling about it. Walking out of the hotel a visitor *would* be followed—this was confirmed a dozen times. It seems so long ago. People tell me now that I wouldn't believe how Riga has changed—so alive and stylish, nothing like the old place I remember. But, appealing as their descriptions are, I have no real desire to update my Soviet-era images. Nor do I really believe that any update would change much for me. Riga was for me long ago plucked from time and sprayed over with some kind of metaphysical fixative. It is, and will remain, an utterly illogical jumble of medieval cobblestones and German baroque detailing and Khrushchev-era prefab, with a beautiful park of bridges, flowers and rolling green dropped into the very center, nothing following as it should on a mere map because every important corner and stretch of sidewalk have been tagged with one or another of my mother's or father's reminiscences—to the point where my walking segues were finally more about time than space, and that the little embankment where someone and someone once sat together abutted directly, maybe even overlapped, the coffee and cake shop where my grandmother met with her friends.

My Riga also contains one sparrow-related anecdote, which I hope can be fitted here like a keystone to join the American and Latvian sides of the story, if "story" is not too grand a term for my extraterritorial meandering.

The last time I traveled there, wanting to save money, I signed up to fly with a charter group composed of American Latvians going to visit relatives. I was in my thirties, married, and I remember how unnerved I was by the idea of having to share a hotel room. I'd been paired up with a man named Viesturs, though when we met in the airport queue he insisted I call him Vic. How disorienting: to be in a small hotel room speaking my intimate, private language—the language that I have pretty much only ever spoken with my family—with a person calling himself Vic, who seemed from our first handshake entirely alien. Once we arrived in Riga, though, I hardly even saw him, except silhouetted a few times in the bathroom doorway late at night after he returned from his latest round of visiting.

I was there to spend some time with my grandmother, who was old and ailing, essentially bedridden. I went to sit with her for several hours every afternoon during the week of my stay. She received me in her bedroom in her ancient-seeming, cluttered, high-ceilinged apartment (where my father had grown up). I would let myself in and then call out to her. I would usually find her lying in her bed with her eyes closed—she had bad cataracts—opening them only to greet me or when she needed to look at notes she had made for my visit. My grandmother had an agenda of things she wanted me to know about. I winced as she brought her scrap of paper so close to her face it almost touched her nose. She had noted down stories about my father as a boy, and herself as a girl or in her courtship days (there was an ill-starred romance at the core of her life), and there were things she'd remembered that she wanted to tell me about writers she had known. Mostly she talked calmly, sequentially, very much the schoolteacher she had been for more than fifty years, but whenever she got on the subject of Peter, my grandfather (and namesake—my middle name is Peter), she would ask me to hold her hand. When she was talking about him, her manner changed completely; her voice became emotional, quavery.

My grandmother could visit with me for only a few hours a day, but she had arranged for me to have a companion for my visit, the grown daughter of one of her old students, Ieva (Eve). I had met her many years before when I had visited Riga with my sister, but I was now shocked to see she had become an attractive young woman. She was—this was also a shock—completely familiar to me. Not so much personally, though we had that slight earlier connection, but . . . genetically. The feeling is hard for me to pin down. It has to do with Latvianness, with the myriad elusive aspects of appearance—skin color, hair, a certain softness in the features—and how these somehow carry over into voice tones, mannerisms, everything. Ieva had a tuned-up shyness that could flare into impetuousness without warning, and even this seemed Latvian to me. She was fresh-faced, with a creamy complexion, and very slightly plump in specific places—the neck, the wrists. What else? I found her witty and responsive, easy to talk to. She had recognized, probably instantly, that she could humor me, and as my Latvian was rough to say the least, she didn't hesitate with the swiftly lifted eyebrow, the wry corrective interventions, the minilectures she conducted with mock seriousness. Within minutes of our meeting again, Ieva had set herself up as my tour guide—for a week she instructed me in her world.

We traversed the beautiful city of Riga in every direction. She pointed, lectured ironically, and flirted. And I flirted back, light and bantering, nothing fraught. How can I explain this? It was the old delightful game, but played in translation. We were busy touring all the places I'd heard about from my parents, the sites of their growing up. Ieva seemed to know all the family stories—she corroborated and explained and told me things I hadn't heard about. Every day we walked, talked, traded our stories, explained ourselves. Except for family, I had never confided anything to anyone in Latvian; I had no ready language for the things I really thought and felt. Maybe for that reason everything I said seemed new to me, itself a new sensation for me.

We had a joke between us. Upon my arrival, playing off my mother's maiden name, she had presented me with a children's book—*Sarezgitais Zvirbulens,* which could be translated to mean "mixed-up little sparrow"—and this became her joke. The cover showed a cartoon rendering of a mussed-up-looking bird. Me. We took our extended tours of the city, and as we went on with our stories she wove that "zvirbulens" theme into everything until it finally became the binding thread of my visit. The mixed-up sparrow on the street corner, dazed in front of the store display, wide-eyed on the trolley. It was all so innocent. Absolutely nothing happened to ground the electricity of those hours except a slightly embarrassed good-bye kiss when it was time for me to leave.

My last visit to Riga remains a beautiful contained memory that has faded to near indistinctness—though as I wrote about it just now, putting words to it for the very first time, I caught a hint of that old sensation. But only a hint. I was like someone touched on the shoulder, almost waking, but then falling back into his dream, though the analogy works better the other way, this being the wakened state, and that, with its aura of old traces and residues, the dream. As such, of course, it is best left alone—not to mention that I am no great believer in dream analyses and interpretations. Except that just this once I feel moved to reflect, though I would proceed not in the Viennese mode, but the Argentinian, à la Borges. I can't help it. The whole memory carries such a strong metaphysical saturation now. I find myself taking up the theme of alternate lives and destinies, playing with the Borgesian idea that as the two of us pursued our tour—through the Old City (itself a kind of dream protruding into the Soviet present), out along the white sands of the Jūrmala shore, crossing this way and that through the park—I was somehow being granted a glimpse of the conjectural life, a picture of how things might have been if the coin had landed tails, not heads: if this and this and this turn had not been taken by my father, my mother, if I had not gotten myself born as who I am, but in what they had grown up believing was the intended place. The bird is part of my conjecturing, the spirit bird, watchful and hovering, ministering to the grains and seeds, moving about in the tangle of all those roots—*sarezgitais zvirbulens* indeed, dazed as I am by the idea of an existence in a whole different world, one that vanished when those other players took their turns.

Grandfather's Painting

The subject matter, a landscape, is one thing, and I'll get to that, but what follows me around—psychologically, I suppose—is a surface of molten yellow-gold that has, year by year, worked its way into my life. How to reach for it? My grandfather was a nature painter who worked mainly on-site, *en plein air* as those light transparent vowels would have it, in Latvia and Russia in his young years, in Germany after the war, and in America, on the grounds of the Booth Estate outside Detroit, in his later life. The Booth Estate, also known as Cranbrook, housed various schools and an art academy, where he, Mike—the name Americanized from Mikhail, his given name—worked installing exhibits and informally coaching painting students. But that's the tail end of a very long story, and the tip of the tail, in a sense, is this painting that I've had for many years now. It depicts a hilly meadow that declines to a lake, which is partly obscured by grand trees, with the roofs of two indistinct buildings placed, if I'm not mistaken, right at the so-called vanishing point. My hesitation makes it clear that I am no expert in the terminology of painting, though that didn't stop me just the other day from launching into a long aside in a writing workshop comparing the essayist's notion of a narrative destination to the painter's marking of that point on his canvas. Here on the canvas the eye is drawn ineluctably to the small reddish-orange oblong, and it happens to be the only trace, in a world otherwise just land, sky, and water, of human presence. Was this a formulated idea? I don't know. I never think of painters as intending things in quite this way, and to be honest, the possibility that Mike might have come to it by way of an idea rather than by pure visual instinct slightly disconcerts me. It wars with the sense of his character—*who he was*—that I had as a child.

The painting, two feet by three, is signed M. A. Zvirbulis in the lower right corner and dated 1960. As he died the very next year, it counts as one of his last. I took possession of it long after, when I began to live away from home—it became part of the very minimal decor of my life. No doubt that's why those colors and hazily rendered shapes are so utterly familiar. I have stared and stared, often without knowing I was staring—which is maybe the real penetration. The landscape hung on nails in the living rooms and bedrooms of so many different apartments before ending up here in our house, where it has sidled from this room to that, finally mounting the dark stairs to come to rest against one of the attic bookcases. This is temporary, I say, and at some point I will give it its right new situation. But the temporary positioning also serves it: for I notice it several times every day when I come up to the attic to work. I mark its glow, or the bit of flat blue that is the lake, in a way I wouldn't if it were to fall back into bewitched slumber on some wall. To be seen a painting has to keep announcing itself; it needs strenuousness, a way to stake its claim over and over. This landscape does many things—to me anyway—but it does not exert itself. Rather, it gives way to the gaze, subsides into itself; it makes no pitch about the world except, unadventurously, that it *is*. But I don't mind. Again and again I contemplate a beautiful vista painted by an artist who loved the look of the world but was also tired, a man for whom seeking serenity had become the first priority.

My attachment to the painting is private, personal. The truth is that I have gradually demoted it over the years, from bedroom to hall to attic, because I don't want people thinking it was the best he could do—there were many finer canvases. Sometimes when my eye surprises it, catches hold of it outside the cloud of my associations, I feel that it sags—formally, I mean. It gives in to its straightforward subject too easily, veers from any raging at the dying of the light. This was, I know, a mark of his character. Mike was thought by many to be too gentle in his responses, too willing to watch the action, whatever action, from a distance. If every family needs a dreamer—and I like to think it does—he was ours. The man was always at a remove, hovering in the middle distance; he was not staring hard at the world, but looking at it as if from over the shoulder, lingeringly.

I take it in: the lake, those trees, the color of what I know to be roofing tiles, these not registered accurately at all, but modified to balance the bright accents in the foreground. I know exactly where he was standing and what he was looking at. Kingswood Lake and the faraway buildings of Kingswood School. I could drive across the country right now, all these decades later, and park by the curb of the wide street that runs between the Art Institute and the Science Museum; I could make my way over the grassy verge and go knee-high right into the grasses to where he stood. I never actually saw him working at that one spot, though I did see him elsewhere. But I know this whole place so well. I passed long seasons of my younger life playing, hiding, and running on the grounds. When I was older I went there to walk or just sit and brood. I crisscrossed that land so often in those years that I have stitched it shut in memory. Nothing can now break into what I remember. I know the wide field and the way it drops away. I hold the grade of the hill in my muscle memory, though the painting jumps right over it, foreshortening the landscape to put the lake just past the wide ridge of brightness. And how odd to think how what to another viewer could just as well be Swabia or Wisconsin or even Norway—a *view*—is to me the most familiar locale in the world. I have the full map, not just the ups and downs of the land, but its intimacy. I know—I knew—where the ground got soft and spongy, and exactly where the geese liked to land and congregate, right by two birch trees, and their tangy goosey smell. I see perfectly the soft hanging stroke lines of the willows by the shore, and I keep in my shoulders, spine, and legs the oblong turning momentum from that patch called Daffodil Hill, which had a slope that made rolling down with arms wrapped around chest irresistible. And, of course, the lake. The painting doesn't show the pebbled path, that carefully landscaped philosopher's walk. Not that anyone ever called it that, but to my mind, maybe even then, it was a metaphysical circuit: once around felt like the distance of a deep thought; twice and you could begin to get somewhere.

Here it is: a painting of a hill and a lake done by an old man, a painter no longer fully in the fray, instead falling back on the consolation of instincts and known moves, moves executed possibly less out of a will to transmit the beautiful world and more because the act of painting itself—the preparation, the first looking and the measuring of distances, the squeezing of pigments onto the palette that always asked for another look, and another—was a way of still holding it close. Brush to paint to canvas—all so long ago. But the canvas now leans against the shelf in my attic and the light he put up keeps traveling.

Fury

I do not know fury, my people do not know fury, fury is not there to be had. Rage yes, bitterness, gall, anger and its thousand satellites—named "irk" and "pique" and "ire"—and certainly all of the modes of deliberate recourse, from vengeance to simple score settling. I see it as a matter of culture, North opposed to South, reason to instinct. Fury is rage erupting into the body, more a passion than an emotion. Fury is the point past which reason cannot intercede, and I can only pine for it. Pine to be the kind of person who is helpless in its torque, who flashes red and feels swept clean when it has run its course. I grew up dreaming that combustion, full of images of the self run riot, yearning for the clarification of release. On the playground at Walnut Lake School, Larry Driver exploding and going after his brother Steve, fists and claws, a scream at the heart of it that terrified the whole group of us, but we could not look away.

Before that, though, there was Wally Morante. This was the summer my sister, Andra, and I stayed with my grandparents at Cranbrook. Wally and his family lived in the downstairs of that little house. It was like a Bavarian cottage, snug, overhung by enormous pines, one of the few places I've been that come back to me with picture-book clarity. Wally was the policeman and gatekeeper of the estate. Handsome and loud. I think of him when I see Marlon Brando in *A Streetcar Named Desire,* only he was Italian, not Polish. Dark skinned and dark eyed in his T-shirts, all chest hair and stubble when he sat out on the steps after work. The same steps I would see him come down every morning clean shaven and wearing his pressed blues. He carried an old-style policeman's hat with a shiny visor; he stood straight and winked at me when he patted his hair before putting it on. I looked at him and I didn't understand. Could this be the same man? What happened? What was it that had him night after night screaming and slamming doors—we heard everything in that little house—shaking our walls with his explosions of "shit" and "fuck" and how he was going to beat his kids—Vince and Artie—until they couldn't stand up? The cry of it filled the house. It started and stopped. And just when it seemed he was finally done it started again. Dorothy, his wife, would make a try at calming him down—her voice came through to us in a placating murmur, barely there—but it was no use. Wally bellowed and slammed and—I'd hear the opening hiss of another beer can—raised his fury to the night sky. Andra and I sat together on the couch upstairs, just the two of us. Where were our grandparents? Try as I might I can't picture them there, though there was no place else they could have been. Noise like this, rage like this, could only end in something terrible. We waited and waited—so many nights, it seemed like something in the world had to change, or break—until we finally fell asleep in it. And then it was morning again, the light so sweet that whole summer, and I played out in front and watched Wally, the handsome policeman, coming down the steps, fresh, giving me a quick wink, both hands reaching up to adjust his hat as he started down the street toward the booth at the main entry.

Lost Things

Lost things have their own special category. So long as they're lost, and felt to be lost, they belong to the imagination and live more vividly than before. They make a mystery. The other day I wanted to write about a tape dispenser—I had a reason—and I searched high and low through the house, checking every place I could think of, until I decided that there are certain things you have to look for by pretending *not* to be looking, or to be looking for something else, in order to *outwit* the inanimate. Using this plan, I walked around pretending to be hunting for . . . a thick rubber band. It didn't work. There were suddenly thick rubber bands everywhere, and not a tape dispenser in sight. Still, I had something I wanted to say. So I sat myself down in the attic and wrote about a tape dispenser without having the object in front of me to study. My description was so detailed as to be overcompensatory, as if I were seeing it more clearly than I could if I had it there on the desk. I rendered it with great exactitude, I thought, doing intimate justice to the inset plastic wheel and the shape of the housing, and differentiating with much care between the construction of the better-grade metal-serrated dispensers and the corner-cutting plastic-edged products you find on sale at high discount. But why was I moved to this writing? It seems I had a story from my young childhood, the memory of an afternoon. I soon discovered myself moving from description to writing about that day when I was six and sitting on the carpet in our living room. I had found a plastic tape dispenser and was completely absorbed in tearing off little strips of tape and attaching them to the leg of the couch. Writing, I remembered the feeling of the room and, strangely amplified, the fascination of adhesion. How was I going to convey these things? It's almost impossible to create tension if you are telling a story about a story—if you are recapping and cutting corners as you go. But I don't want to let this go.

I'm in the living room playing, and my younger sister, Andra, is with me. Or she must have been, because when the drama started she was right there, part of everything. My mother is nearby, busy. She is hurrying to go out somewhere, and moving the way she does at these times: many small actions, the close and faraway sound of her shoes in the hall. She is anxious. She has always been a restless, fidgety person, and getting ready to do anything always brings her to a pitch. She has been calling to us over and over to get ready. And though I'm immersed in my occupation, tearing off bits of tape, working, I'm also tracking the sounds, judging the urgency, calculating how soon I will really have to stop my project—which is, of course, gaining in fascination the closer she is to having to go. As the anxiety increases—faster clicks of her heels, a sharper inflection in her voice: *Stop playing now and get ready, we're going*—so does my reluctance. I feel myself refusing her. Why do I do this? I'm old enough to know how my mother gets when she is pushed too far—so frustrated and helpless acting and so close to tears that I'll do anything to make her feel better. But this afternoon I go on with tearing my tape. And though her calls to us are getting sharper, more exasperated, I don't stop. I pull the strips of clear tape and tear them off neatly, fixing each one to the leg of the couch.

This one time, though, I've read the moment wrong. Enough really *is* enough, but I haven't noticed. I'm hunched over my toy, playing my baiting game, when—I replay it now like a scene from a horror movie—a violent shape comes whooshing down into my circle, a hand with talons, reaching for the dispenser in my hand, and grabbing harder when I clutch at it, finally *tearing* it from me. And then suddenly it's like an egg breaking, except blood. Red color everywhere, and screaming—my mother, my sister, me. My mother yanks my hand into the light—and then freezes. We all see it: a big meaty section of my fingertip—of me— is hanging loose. I don't know if it hurts, or what I should think. I don't know anything. I'm dead-centered in a terrible, but also thrilling, whirl of things: towels and calling on the telephone and rushing to the car, me sitting in the big front seat holding my hand, my finger, all wrapped in my lap while my mother drives to the doctor's. This last part I'm guessing. My visual memory actually stops short at the sight of the fingertip. The rest is without picture—it's all feeling. Wonderful feeling: my mother's rage pulled inside out. I have her stroking my forehead and saying how she's sorry, sorry, sorry. Whatever I did wrong has been stripped away. Everything seems light. I am more blameless than I've ever been.

This was the story I was writing the other day, though of course I told it differently. When I had finished, when I had gone back through it, scrolling back and forth, like I always do, trying to get it just right, the balance of parts, the rhythm, I highlighted it to copy and I hit another command—to paste, I thought—but God knows what I did because the whole thing vanished in an eye blink. As though it had never existed. Suddenly there was nothing. Just like that. I was staring at a white screen, a blinking cursor. Of course I tried every strategy I could think of to recover it. I even called my savvy fourteen-year-old to come up to help me—and he tried—but the piece really was gone. I was undone. I felt myself rattling with the loss. I thought: I should dive in right away and rewrite while everything was still fresh, but I didn't have the heart. Was the memory really that important? Maybe not. I suddenly went back to the day two years earlier when I methodically deleted, file by file, the hundreds of pages of a novel I had been working on for a very long time. It was failing me, I was failing it. I intended my decision to be a liberation, a truncation made for the sake of the rest of my work. I remember my decisiveness. Hitting the button again and again felt consequential. One last stroke: I was done. There were no more files to delete. When everything was at last gone I sat there. And then I caught up with myself. I was stunned. I had overdone it—I saw that right away. It was not just the pages that were gone, I realized, but everything they represented—those hundreds, no, thousands, of hours, and all that had led up to them, all the walking and brooding—everything had been sucked out backward through the keyhole and rendered null.

Beside this, the loss of the tape-dispenser memory was trivial. It had only been a few pages long, and I still had most of the images and phrases in my head. If I wanted I could get it back. *If I wanted.* But just then I didn't—I logged off and closed my laptop.

Two minutes later I was downstairs heading toward the kitchen. On my way through the hall I happened to look down. There, on the little red table by the door, on its side, distinct as a medallion in a museum display, sat the plastic dispenser I'd been searching for. A wink from the gods. I didn't even shake my head when I saw it. But in that split second I knew: this piece here has to be a parable, a koan of some kind. A lost object is used as the basis of a narrative, then the narrative disappears—becomes a lost object—and then the object itself reappears, lodging in the writer's mind, so that he knows right away that he has to tell his story again, only this time carefully folding it up in a story *about* the story. As if thus to keep it safe.

Schimmelpenninck

Schimmelpenninck: Made in Holland. A dented little tin taken down from
the cluttered top shelf of the bookcase behind my attic desk, a bookcase
that has become one of my default reliquaries, like the sieve in the kitchen
drain that catches the washup of a family meal, except that the sieve then
gets emptied into the kitchen trash while the sentimental refuse of living
just accumulates. I picked it up in the spirit of "you have to start somewhere," but also with a certain confidence. I am, after all, the writing
teacher who quotes to his students the line from Flaubert: "Anything becomes interesting if you look at it long enough." And I do believe it, interest being the discovery of connections that feel as if they are *leading*
somewhere, marking a path. Interest is the product of attention. Look!
Look closer! What do you see? Start with the eye and find out what happens. Pray, as Lowell did, for the grace of accuracy.

Schimmelpenninck. Well, the little tin is there to be looked at, but it
would be nothing to me—sentimentally, associatively—if it weren't for
the sound and look of that word. A word that is absolutely empty of
meaning for me. A brand of cigarillos, yes. A little choo-choo train of
m's and n's. Just above the script on the tin a small inset image of a high-
browed and peruked gentleman with a stiff collar and a formal-looking
flow of white cloth, almost a bib, where a tie would ordinarily go. Herr
Schimmelpenninck? Or is this the king of Holland offering his imprima-
tur on the product? It could just as well be Goethe, there's that same projection of entitled nobility. The whole effect—and probably the reason I
kept the thing—is very haute European. And I know where this fine and
twisty thread leads. Back to the drawer of my father's desk, upstairs in our
old house in Michigan. That desk, its top right drawer I realize now also a
reliquary, was a regular stop for me as I made my way through the rooms.
Alone, bored—it seems I was both for years at a stretch—I snooped and
sifted through every cranny of my parents' lives, looking for God knows

what, a confirmation or denial, maybe the concealed document testifying to my true origins, I don't think it mattered *what,* only that I had the feeling that there was something to be found. As if in the scattered stuff of my parents' lives lay the secret, the missing card that completed the deck.

I never found it, but my charged-up idle investigating brought me right up against all sorts of things—I mean literal *things,* bundled letters, peculiar artifacts of completely mysterious provenance, like a tiny elephant figurine, and an ancient cigarette lighter that I was clumsy in disassembling— that I broke—and that had my father confronting me in a fury. *How dare I? Did I have any idea what that meant?* This was a lighter he had found during the war, while he was making his way from one place to another, escaping. He wouldn't tell me the story—he added it to the pile of things he would one day explain about his life. I nodded solemnly and promised to leave his things alone, knowing as I did that I would be back, only more careful. For I was right! These objects of theirs, throughout the house, but in this drawer especially, were soaked in significance; they held clues. At least some of them did. But which ones? Without the stories I couldn't guess. So I had to imagine everything as a possible clue. I can hear the sound of that drawer rolling open. And there was the tin of Schimmelpennincks. With real cigarillos in it, just under the stiff waxy paper. Maybe a few missing. I can picture my father lighting one in the late evening, with a whisky drink. Though really he smoked cigarettes, a few a day—his Benson & Hedges in their elegant khaki-green box, also there in the drawer. The Schimmelpennincks must have been a gift. From a client, a European friend. They had that air. I probably took one out and put it between my lips, then carefully replaced it. Much as a girl might try out just a bit of her mother's lipstick. We want to pretend. Really we want to get in close, as close as we can.

But this tin here, my tin, is not that. I can't remember how I came by it, but I know it was not from my father. I may have bought it during one of my attempts to quit smoking, figuring I could allow myself one cigarillo a day, my reward for restraint. If I bought them—I'm pretty sure I did, from Leavitt & Peirce in Harvard Square, back when I worked down the street at the bookstore—I would have done so both for the association and because the cigarillos themselves were the length and basic shape of cigarettes. Enough about that. There are other things about the tin. The fact that there are things *in* it. When I picked it up from the shelf earlier I heard a tumble of metal sound. Coins. And maybe something else. But I wasn't holding my breath. I have little gangs of pennies everywhere. Pennies flock to me. I empty my pockets at the end of the day and leave them on the nearest surface, and when the clutter gets to me, I sweep them into jars and tins. Nothing unique here. The Schimmelpenninck is just another container with stray pennies. Not like that little box—and where on the crowded planet is it now?—the cache all through my childhood for my Indian Head pennies. What aura they had—and what a thrill it would be if they suddenly turned up somewhere.

I put the tin on the desk in front of me and opened it to confirm. I was right. Pennies, pennies . . . and a button, the kind you clip to your lapel, with a rainbow design and the words *Mikrofons* and *Aptauja* and the number 81. And a neatly folded scrap of thin beige-salmon paper that I recognize instantly as Latvian. I have never seen paper of this color and consistency anywhere else. The button I place right away—a small souvenir from a trip I took to Latvia, by myself, in the early 1980s. *Mikrofons* refers to a pop radio station in Riga, I think, and *Aptauja*—here is one of the many words that marks the line of my outsiderness. I grew up speaking Latvian at home, I remain moderately fluent—older Latvians often remark on it with surprise—but there must be thousands of words like this one, *Aptauja*, that I just don't know. And because of these words I feel at a permanent remove, lacking some secret password, just like I remember feeling back on the playground when kids used tags and phrases I hadn't learned yet. How did they know to be yelling "batterbatterbatter" so confidently at our recess games? I mouthed the syllables but felt completely exposed.

Finally, that scrap of paper. Unfolding it, I see that it's a ticket: *Andreja Upisa LPSR Valsts Akademiskais Dramas Teatris.* The theater. Stamped for October 10, 1982. I remember being taken to a play, but I keep not a hint of anything that might have happened on the stage, though I do have a secondary sense memory, a small cloud of feeling: the space was plush, baroque feeling; the lights were warm. And I know that when I later read Chekhov's "Lady with a Lapdog," when Gurov travels to the provinces to find Anna and attends the theater—where he first sees her again—this theater is what I picture. But then everything I read of Russian literature is in some way embellished by my Latvian exposures, whether these be my memories of being in Riga at different times—the feeling of my grandmother's dark stairwell, the look of windows and sills, the Slavic faces at kiosks—or my own imaginings projected into the stories I heard growing up, from my parents, but more richly from my grandmother Um, who had such a store of exotic memories from her life, and who trumped my other tellers by reaching farther back: her tales of the farm, of trains and soldiers, held the real redolence.

Set against those stories of Um's, their reach into the timeless time when things had weight and the world was how it had been forever—not changing every minute—1982 is nothing at all. And for a long time it wasn't. What happened? I close my eyes, open them again: 1982 is as far away as a lit auditorium in Riga in what was still the Soviet era, marked for me most clearly now by that off-textured paper with its date and place, which I have just now refolded along its creases and replaced in its Schimmelpenninck tin.

Head

The size of my fist, or maybe a young owl, an owlet, nice in the hand, exactly the thing that if the house were on fire I would grab on the way out—this white head, sculpted from clay and glazed shiny, one of my daughter Mara's high school art class projects. It's an old man's face, fashioned with much thumb pressure, one here for the cheekbone, another here, eyes pressed shut under a strong shapely ridge for the eyebrows, between them a Roman senator's nose, and a mouth that is—depending on your angle and the light—either a disgusted sneer or a harelip. It's beautiful. It *speaks*. I remember the day she brought it home from her school art show and told me that if I liked it so much I could have it. That was a few years ago. The thing has been on my desk ever since, perched in my peripheral vision. In summer, when the wind blows through the attic windows, it may do duty as a paperweight, but otherwise it just sits there, shining at me every time I turn to the right. So I have slowly taken it in, absorbed it, puzzling again and again not only over its likeness but also the idea of likeness itself, how it is that a few well-placed bumps and indentations can add up to something more than the baseline notion of a face—how they take on an undeniable psychological reality. Projection, I tell myself. The very same thing that turns a drop cloth and a clump of rope into a large yellow dog sleeping near the oil burner in the basement. What amazes me is not so much that I should make an image from available shapes, but that I should do it in a mere instant, and that the image should be so precise—*and* that it should so often have a story with it. Imagination works in a flash: how the dog found its way in, why it should be sleeping so abjectly, what we will do with it. But then I take another step forward and it's gone. And now this little head, a Roman senator one day, Ozymandias the next. The great shattered stone figure of Shelley's sonnet, whose lips hold a "sneer of cold command"—a poem I cannot think of, ever, without remembering the night I sent my sister, Andra, into a panic of crying that I could not talk her back from. "Don't you see?" I was cruel, insistent, trying out my nihilism. I must have been fourteen or so, she eleven. "Don't you get it? There is nothing." I told her the news. "We live and we die. And this poem says it all." *Round the decay / Of that colossal wreck, boundless and bare / The lone and level sands stretch far away.* There was no taking it back after the words were out. Myself, I was inured: to me this was old news. I was too young to realize that old news wakens into new news time and again, and when it does there is nothing to be done.

If I turn my friend just a quarter turn, though, Ozymandias shades back into the dour Roman, or—I think of this only now!—a stand-in for the Etruscan, that bland crude tufa shape that stared at all of us—the family—from its slit in the brick wall by the patio. I know there was a story about its acquisition—there is always a story—but I forget. Andra and I were still kids. My parents unpacked their suitcases after a long trip and placed a bundle of newspaper on the bed. We stood by, as we always did when they got back from their travels, waiting for presents. This was not a present, but we were curious. We watched as our father opened the bundle sheet by sheet to reveal—a white stone head. Ugly, basic flat features, gaping nothing eyes. "Etruscan!" he announced. The Etruscans, he said, were in Italy long before the Romans—they were the first people. The face corroborated that. It was dull and distant and pocky with holes. "I have a good place for it," he said. And for twenty-plus years it brooded there, grown into its niche, battered looking and vacant in the day when I passed it on the way to the drive or coming in with groceries, but more than a little unnerving if I ever stepped out onto the patio at night. There are things I'll never get used to. Like the sudden jolt of that shape, not a face but an aura, stark as the night, no link at all to the world I've drawn around me, to the glow of light at the side windows, the long drapes rippling in front of the open sliding door.

Mara is an artist, I think. Or she was when she put her fingers and thumbs to that clay, and when she later cut her initials—MB—on the back of the head. An artist—like her great-grandfather Mike, Mikhail, who will forever be the template of that for me, in whom I glimpsed—or felt—for the very first time that twist of self or soul that takes a person a half step away from the business of others. Who knows why that happens or how that works? Trained in Moscow at the academy, he painted beautifully—landscapes mainly. He died when I was eleven, still in grade school, but by then I had already marked it: there was something in him that ran on its own clockwork. He would be sitting with the rest of us at family dinner, partaking, but also not, and if I didn't quite understand back then, I do now. Though of course I romanticize. The artist!

If Mike is in my thoughts right now, it's through another connection, different but related. Everything relates. A few years before he died, when he was less and less often taking his paints and easel out to the lake at Cranbrook where he had painted for so many summers, my parents asked Mike if he would make large oil portraits of my sister and me. He was not a portrait painter—he had never done much with the human figure or likeness—but he agreed.

I don't remember much about this. If either of us "sat" for him it was only briefly—he worked mainly from photographs. I never saw him put paint to those canvases, but I know he completed a large painting of my sister that he was not at all happy with. Neither were my parents. There must have been some delicate deliberations. What to do? Do we hang it because it's Mike, or—? The painting finally disappeared into our old upstairs closet, and I haven't seen it for decades. I should ask where it is now. My portrait was never finished. Mike sketched my face on a large canvas and then stopped. But this time he got something. My mother and father both said so—they loved the drawing. It was taken right from my third-grade school picture. But it was art—it came to life. The lines made by hand were for some reason deeper or truer than what the camera had captured. There was my face, floating in the middle of the big canvas. Still, though everybody urged him on, Mike would not finish it.

If the project dead-ended, the image has stayed. My mother cut out and framed the face, that first beginning, and it hung on the wall in my parents' bedroom in Michigan for the next forty years. I have only to close my eyes and I see it there surrounded by family photos. My parents have since moved. Now the "portrait" hangs on the wall of my mother's study in their new condominium. A testament to something. To projections, or to what would be their opposite: excavations. She sees it there, that work of an afternoon, every time she looks to the left from the little desk where she writes cards and pays bills.

Wink

A wink. The slightest scrim between the worlds—though maybe it's not a scrim or a curtain so much as a split-second flash between things, closer to the action of a camera click, exposure. But while the movement itself is enacted in a fraction of a second, it needs the situation, the setup, to give it sense. In this case it needs Arnis. Arnis was a Latvian friend of my parents', one of those adults who was always promoting himself as a kind of uncle, though there was no link of relation. I think he just liked the leverage of that familiarity. With me, my sister, but maybe with other kids in other families, too. I don't know. He was one of those adults I saw only rarely, at those Latvian gatherings we occasionally attended, at the big annual Song Festival when it was held in Cleveland or Chicago, where he lived, or at the car rallies my father and a few of his friends went to for a period of time—my father and his friend August raced; Arnis was an onlooker. And every so often he would just appear. I would come home from school and see an unfamiliar car in the drive, and there he would be in the living room with a drink and a cigarette, talking with my mother. I always felt I was intruding midconversation, interrupting something that had its roots in the other world—Latvia, Germany—and was now leafing out in the smoke from his cigarette. Sometimes he would stay for dinner; other times he would look at his watch and hitch up his slacks from the knee and say that he needed to be on his way. The only other occasion I remember, from those early days, is when I came out from school one afternoon and saw him and my mother standing together on the sidewalk. This was somehow different. Arnis was wearing dark sunglasses and had his hair combed back, like a sport, a player, words I didn't know, of course. What might have come to mind was that old one-liner, "Kookie, Kookie, lend me your comb," which referred to the character on the TV show *77 Sunset Strip* who was forever combing back his hair. Why were Arnis and my mother standing out in front of Walnut Lake School? If they said, I don't remember. Though I do remember he went into the store across the street on some errand, and my mother and I waited. Then we all drove home together. I'm implying nothing here, and suggesting only that he was different from my parents' other friends. He didn't have that same adult solidity, even though he was married and worked in some engineering-related profession. But he dressed more like those smooth bachelor characters you saw in movies, and he was quick to freshen his drink—I noticed that—or start in on his beer before the head had settled. So much for background. What I always come back to with Arnis is the wink. That one instant of memory stands out, though the scene around it is a bit blurry. There was a table, a sunlit room—in our house, or at my parents' friends' house in Chicago when we visited—and a room full of adults, all talking. And Arnis was saying something, telling a story, a joke, maybe, and he had people listening. It was clear to me that he was building toward something—a punch line, some twist or revelation—when I came into the room. I preserve this moment, my sense of imminence, because I got the very distinct feeling that Arnis felt me step into the room. Though he didn't turn to look, I felt the smallest shift, a hesitation, a kind of stutter in the air. This makes me think, all these decades later, that the story was not for kids. But he didn't stop. There was that slight catch, and then we went on talking. This fits with my sense of his character—that showmanship, the desire to get his effect, his response, would trump any considerations about what a kid might hear. He set it all up, dropped his clincher—Arnis was a great wielder of the abruptly innocent expression—and everyone laughed. I imagine adults in a half circle, ice melting in their drinks, and of course that's how it would have been, that's how it was. The one thing I'm not guessing about, though, what's vivid as can be in memory, is the way he turned—turned as though he knew right where I stood—gave me a measuring look, and winked. It happened just like that. I saw the flash of lid, and then I caught the look behind it, an adult look, one that said: you know what I'm talking about, or if you don't you soon will—this is how things really are. Welcome.

Old Glasses

. . . and, oh, what's this? Up here, in the kitchen, high on the shelf that serves as the cemetery of unclassified items—the rubber-banded clutch of expired passports, the unidentified pills that could be just the needed thing if we were sure what they were, checkbook ledger inserts going back at least three years . . . My hand closes around a leatherette oblong, the glasses case—embossed *Lenscrafters*—for my emergency pair, which could still, under the right set of circumstances, be a lifesaver. Almost everything that gets saved—in this house, in my life—falls under that anxious rubric "under the right set of circumstances." The "what if?" Or else it goes into the sentiment file. I mean, why else hold on to the passports? Only because *anything* that was kept in the pocket for that long, in that many different places, can't just be disposed of. But never mind, it's the glasses I want now—those smudged, gnawed-looking things that look as if they belong with rings and wallet in an effects envelope at the morgue. But they were for a few years—and not that long ago, either—part of the presentation package. Me offering my face to the world, me *seen* by the world: bespectacled, nappy-headed creature. The styling of glasses indicates so much. These—wire rims, oval lenses—say what? Serious man, not too many frills, I don't know. But they mean *some*thing. Looking at them here in my hand I run the time-lapse montage of me putting them on, day after day—first finding them, of course, the blind fingers tapping the likely places near the bedside, then reflexively opening the "legs" and mounting the bridge like a saddle over the nose, not merely *putting on* glasses, but in fact admitting the world that comes with them. Because without this little contraption of wire and molded plastic I am worse than visually incapacitated; I am humanly helpless. And, frankly, foolish—a grown man batting at what he knows to be cereal boxes on top of the refrigerator, feeling in the cutlery drawer for a spoon, and bringing a plastic container right up to his face to make sure it holds milk.

I've been this way since the third grade. Fifty years, but I still remember putting on that first pair, how the ground—terra firma—all of a sudden drew away and wavered. I was the stranger in a strange land, a stilt man. I wanted to cry. My romantic prospects, not great to begin with, went to nil. There was the long period of taking them off and putting them on through the long school day, anything so Robin Greeson wouldn't see them on my face. Nor would I wear them in class photos. They were conspicuous, ugly. I felt that, and I was right. Then one afternoon a group of us were lined up in Shawn Sweeney's yard throwing snowballs at passing cars, which was great fun—until I scored a direct windshield hit and the driver stopped. The man jerked himself out of the car so fast that I panicked, frozen in my spot. He stood with his hand on the open door and looked right at me—he had me dead to rights. I was sure he was going to come running after me. But no. He raised his arm instead. "Next time I'll get you!" he yelled. He pointed at me. "I know you—four eyes." *Four eyes.* I'd never heard the phrase before. It was utterly preposterous. But the words had jumped right to his lips, so they had to be true.

That was the last of the struggle. After that the glasses stayed on, became the new constant. Only the prescription changed, every few years, the styling. Otherwise, there was nothing much to think about. People used to talk about taking your glasses off before you got in a fight, but I never fought. Or else before you kissed, but kissing was beyond a pipe dream, at least for another decade. By the time kissing happened I had shed every last memory of my unadorned presence. I was the person who fit the world to his face every morning and set it aside at night, with ceremonial intervals in between, carefully controlled, when he took the things off, steamed them with a hot breath, and rubbed them clean. Honestly—I don't know who I am without my glasses. When I take them off and look in the mirror, I can't see myself. Not really. And if I lean in too close to the glass I start to feel crazy, like I've become my father. This might have something to do with how I felt as a kid when I saw the man without *his* glasses. In his pajamas brushing his teeth, or sitting up from a nap on the couch. I took in all that hollow space around his eyes. Why did that make him so different? Then, a few years back, a photographer from a magazine insisted on shooting me barefaced. Intrigued, I let him. The photo ran and it troubles me even now to think of it. When I saw that person's picture I wanted to help him—help him find his chair, cross the street, get through the rest of his life. "Here, put these on. They're glasses."

And what about these, the old ones? They're just sitting here, incomplete, wanting something. If not a face, then maybe one final writerly twist. Every instinct is saying *Put them on! Say how things look through those old eyes!* But I just can't do it. I take one good look at the discolored plastic nosepieces, notice the tiniest flecks of white paint spattered on a lens, and I know exactly how strange everything would be if I made the switch: I can already feel the jarring unease of a world slightly "off" . . . And I also know how easy it would be to turn that into some big artistic correlative.

Schoolroom

I had the feeling of what I wanted, but I didn't have the prompt, the sliver, the bit of grit that grows the pearl, but then I lay down to nap and there they all were, gathered up as if for a group photograph, though nothing that frontal or formal. Still, the scene was all there. I saw the milky white backs of necks and the corncobbed pencils and those black rubber boots with cross-clips, open to the schoolroom heat and dripping on the linoleum. In one slow take I had all the echelons of that old intimacy: the desk and chair rooted on their gray plugs, the hinged desktop angled down over the wide scooped metal interior, the sweet-smelling varnish that was such a promise on the first day, when the books were still stacked neatly in the bin and the thumb traced back and forth slowly in the smooth wide groove cut into the front desk edge. These occasions of absolute renewal—the ache of them still comes back for a moment every year, a sensation never completely lost. Walnut Lake School. September. The floors polished, the blackboards fresh-clean, the chalks lined up unbroken. Legs and feet meet up with this year's desk and chair, heels tucking back right away to find the rung, knees pushing up hard to test the metal. Only when the first space has been mastered does the attention start to inch itself gradually outward, to those white necks, the shirts and blouses, stopping over and over to graze, to take in the whorls of fine hair, bumps on the wrists, the profiles of those sitting on either side. The yearlong daydream begins.

The gaze is like water, flowing out and over, but slowly. And never again is it so alert and undivided. The teacher is talking. We are learning about the esophagus, about the Andes, but against that faraway drone, moving as if over and above, the eye searches out whatever at the moment most compels: the tendon actions of my fingers as they stretch and lightly drum the desktop, the tinny sprawl of bracelet charms against that girl's wrist. *That* girl . . . Karen Middleton—I name her instantly now, though I haven't thought of her for almost half a century. She had Raggedy Ann–colored hair and freckles and almost shiny white skin, and I studied her only because she was there, right next to me, even as I knew, I did, that she was one of the tribe that was not my tribe. By what cues do we know these things? Karen Middleton, that hair and those freckles, so clear to me, but in that clarity standing for all the people I have moved among and never connected with.

We sift our affinities mysteriously. How happy I would have been if I had even one year drawn a desk beside or at least with a good angle on Robin Greeson, who every September was seated so far across the room as to not be in the same class at all. Nearness is everything. Robin was either head-bendingly at the back, in some queen's corner of her own, or else right up by the teacher, ready to catch any pencil that might roll off her desk. If I could only have swapped Robin with Karen—Robin of the bangs and plaid ribbons and shined-up loafers, of the smooth pale legs bracketed between skirt and knee socks. But she was never positioned to be my study. Maybe that was just as well, or so I made myself think for years, even long after the time when I should have forgotten her name. Because whatever pull I felt toward her, Robin never really took me in. I was as sure of this as I was of my feelings, my *lack* of feelings, for Karen Middleton. Robin's inner radar was, of course, fixed on a boy named Steve. Steve was tall, good-looking, relaxed, the natural captain for any team. Because I so admired him I just *assumed* that Robin did, too.

But no. Some of the eye-opening shocks of my life have been the things I learned long after they had any supposed mattering left in them. Like in this case what I heard from my college love, Sally, who as it happened had been in all those same rooms with me (another story), a fellow watcher, as intent on her business as I was on mine. And when we got together so many years later, we were naturally compelled to go back to it all. It was our game, our ongoing joke—*My God, I can't believe you remember that*—returning to those rooms, bringing up those deep and sometimes poisonous alliances, the affronts, all the blurting embarrassments, and in the process inadvertently rescripting some of my most basic assumptions. Sally had her own special access, and an instinct for signals invisible to me. So it was that she was able to widen her eyes at me one night ten or more years after Walnut Lake and say, *Are you serious?* We were talking about Robin and Steve. *She couldn't* stand *him!* She may have said more, she probably did. But I tuned out as I felt that old world start to turn on a new axis. Such a silly scrap of information, really, but it showed me how much I had not understood, it marked the scope. I wanted to haul myself off to a lair where I could be alone to nurse the implications. Of Robin never liking Steve (so casually mentioned) and—in fact there *was* more—actually quite liking me. *Me!* Why, that changed everything—my whole sense of myself down through the years! I waited then for the news to catch up. Waited and waited. But it never did. I was just where I was, nothing altered. The shape of things had been set, long set, much of it in those early rooms, back in the time of keenest attention. Hostage at my desk, drumming with my heels against the metal crossbar of my chair, I had been taking in the whole larger world, its steady immediacy, the look and feel of its ordinary things, absorbing its people the way they need to be absorbed, slowly, layer by layer, starting there with the white band of skin above that girl's collar.

The Friend

I'm reading the bound galleys of a book called *Failure,* a memoir pitched around its title theme. In the chapter I just finished, the writer, Josh Gidding, remembers being at Exeter and falling too readily under the sway of a smart and sardonic classmate, regarding it now as one of the many ways in which he didn't come up to scratch. I've been making my own connections left and right. Just pages before, Gidding was mocking himself as an aspiring intellectual, a pipe-smoking poseur whose most vivid literary attachment was to the character of Rupert Birkin in D. H. Lawrence's *Women in Love,* the very same fixation I'd very recently written about. We even cited the same line from the novel, Birkin's saying to Ursula Brangwen, "I don't believe that." Ursula has just announced that love between a man and woman is absolute, admits no others. Birkin, we know, is thinking about his great friend Gerald Crich, which I mention because these feelings are such a part of this other thing, this "falling under the sway" business. For me it was my friend of late high school and then college years, Todd Wagner, who christened himself "Reddog" in 1969 after we went to Woodstock together, and who has never been anything but Reddog since to me.

What struck me so sharply as I read was the realization that I've gone for years without giving my old friend, the whole life of our friendship, more than a passing nod. For such a long time he was the very center of things, a constant reference point in my inner life, a figure of—I knew it even then—disproportionate influence. It's been decades since we've seen each other, and though I know he lives in New York, I'm never really tempted to look him up when I visit the city. This is not just because we would have little besides the past in common—I'm sure we're very different—but also because I like to think I'm psychologically done with him. I don't really want to be reminded of the times, of myself in those times, when I wasn't.

This is a hard story to tell in strict sequence. What I have now are impressions, memory's quick jump cuts from first contact, when he was the short-haired new boy just arrived at Cranbrook from a military academy in Indiana, to his quick entry into our self-consciously artsy little group of smokers, to my going over to his house for some reason after school, sitting on his narrow attic bed while he played me his Buffalo Springfield and Velvet Underground albums. We started spending time together, and somehow he became, along with Brad Anthony, my great friend for that whole long period—through senior year and then on into college, when we all went to Ann Arbor together. Though he and Brad never clicked, there was a pretense of trying, part of my early schooling in the endless shuttle diplomacy of friendship.

Reddog was thin, fairly tall, flat-bodied, and people were always remarking to me how good-looking he was, as if I needed to know. I got that, but only later. When he first joined our group he hadn't grown out his short military hair, and his features seemed strangely prominent to me. This all changed with long hair and then, in college, his mustache and beard—he really *was* good-looking. I saw how girls—women—turned his way when we were out somewhere, but I still couldn't get all the way past that first impression. The other issue was intelligence. He was smart, got good grades, did his work, but I never felt that he was a serious thinker, or wanted to be. His way with ideas seemed straightforward, unsurprising. Though possibly I was just looking for some point of advantage.

I start with these negatives, these reservations, because I'm trying to figure out where his power came from. For me it was not about looks or smarts, but something more psychological. There was some way he *enlisted* me almost right away, and from that time on he had power over me. And in my deep-down, mostly concealed way I capitulated to him. What was it? I wanted to please him, I feared his scorn, and maybe, too, I sensed some brittle fragility in him that I was always trying to protect. This same impulse, I realize now, defined much of how I acted around my father during all my years of growing up. There's no sorting it all out, not past a point, not here. I'm more focused right now on the influence, its duration, how it was there in my life as a given from senior year, through the first years of college, and how it faded away only in my junior year, when I got involved with Sally. But all those days and nights when Reddog and I hung out together, he at my place, I at his, stoned or not—it was all like some test I was trying to pass, an admissions exam for I don't know what. For me that was what it was about, at some level, our jokes and doings and conversations aside. If I could stop playing to Reddog, stop caring about his reactions, if I could somehow get to where he had no power over me, then I would know I had finally arrived. But why was that? Did I see him as the holder of the keys to some ultimate property? I don't think so. No, what makes all this so strange, so fascinating to me, is that I saw his flaws and fallibilities and weaknesses, but relented to him anyway.

There were two qualities that combined in Reddog's character. One was that he possessed a deep, seemingly absolute nihilistic alienation, which makes perfect sense given how he began to act later, and the other, maybe connected, was that he had the courage of his singularity, his absurdity. In a time when so many of us were secretly cowed by our ideas of what was and was not hip, Reddog took the high ground. He proclaimed himself the arbiter of his own attitude, and that was that.

I start to remember things now: his high crazy laugh, something you might hear echoing in the corridors of an asylum, and then the way he would get giddy and start hammering the table with his palm, people in bars or restaurants turning their heads. And I can see his big hoop earring (I had never known a man to wear such a thing), and his long camel-colored overcoat and lace-up combat boots—the manic way he would stride along the streets of Ann Arbor. Then he was with beautiful Anna, his tall, dark-haired Polish girlfriend our freshman year—and I was eaten up with jealousy. Later, after that first year in the dorm, he moved away from the rest of us, took a room in the Downtown Club, Ann Arbor's transient hotel. That struck us all as a bold move. I would drop in afternoons to find him reading Lawrence Durrell, smoking his Camels, his pot. He made tea for himself and walked around in some kind of Indian wrap. I felt myself starting to lose contact. And in my junior year things got edgy. He didn't get on with Sally. Or any woman I knew. I tried to bring them together but got so nervous I couldn't talk. I never knew what was coming next. Laughing, but not really, he would suddenly start calling women "bitches" and "cunts," aggressive throw-down words that sliced between us and always put me in the position of having to spin what he said, or joke it away, or explain later to whomever I was with that he wasn't really like that. But he was.

At some point, midcollege, Reddog decided that he would become a painter. He stayed with it, sketching and sketching in his room. To see him you had to go to his place and find him. As soon as he graduated he rented a garage on a side street away from campus and bought rolls of canvas and spent every day in his T-shirt and torn jeans, making his huge paintings. He imitated Oskar Kokoschka at one point, I remember. Big blotchy portraits. It was also obvious that he had started to drink. Whenever I stopped by the garage to visit he would be putting paint to canvas or taking it off with his palette knife, or stepping back in a self-conscious squinting mockery of the possessed painter, holding up his thumb as if weighing proportions, studying lines of force. The Camel was always burning in the saucer; there was always an open beer nearby. I felt it was my job not only to take the painting seriously, to walk back and forth and comment, but to endorse the whole enterprise, to convey my admiration and envy for this mighty romantic splurge. I did my best, but I also stopped going every day. And then? I must have begun relocating the deep center of my life, because things get blurry and I lose track.

At some point, I know, Reddog closed up shop and moved to Florida. To earn money, to work, to be with another of his women. The name Sandy suddenly comes back to me—twenty years and I suddenly remember Sandy. She was another of his tough beauties, and I know from stories he told me later that she gave him a run for his money. They rented a trailer in Florida and, the way Reddog told it, drank and painted and fought. When did I first realize what the whole business was about? That Reddog was living a movie, screening himself: the mad unpredictable bohemian, the beatnik pirate (he had studied his Kerouac, Ginsberg, Burroughs,

Bowles); then the painter, the madcap Rothko, Pollock, de Kooning . . . ?
By the time he got to Florida the painting reel had begun to run out, and
the drinking intensified.

I wind forward now. I'm back from living in Maine—Sally and I are long
broken up—and I'm living with my new girlfriend, Pam, in an airless
top-floor apartment with a fire escape. I'm doing my own movie (heart-
break kid, writer to be), but of course I don't see that. This is when Reddog
emerges from somewhere out of the historical blue. He's in town, at loose
ends. He comes to find me in the bookstore where I work. He leads with
the old bravado, gesturing and carrying himself like he's full of legend—
but I see right away that he's more tired looking. "Rough," as my mother
would say. I remember thinking that it's starting to get late for him, that
he may not be able to pull off whatever trick he's trying.

The drinking is even more obvious now. One time comes back clearly.
Pam and I have some people over. It's a summer night and we're all crowded
together out on the fire escape. When Reddog arrives he's already drunk,
fired up. Right away he fixates on Pam's friend Sara and starts up his routine, an exaggerated kind of sweet talk with a suggestion of something
dark just under it, like Treat Williams in that movie *Smooth Talk,* which
I remember only because I got such a strong sense of Reddog when I
watched it recently, right down to physical resemblance. But Sara is not
falling for whatever he's trying, and Reddog is raising the stakes, acting more outrageous, shouting out things in a way that makes people at
the party stop their conversations. What then? I don't remember any sequence, just that at one point he was out of control, screaming, throwing
bottles, and that my feeling about him felt changed in a way that I knew
could not be changed back.

But I don't want to end on such a bleak note. Memory loops around and
around, and good things aren't that easily erased. Also, there were a few con-
tacts after that let me see his life had gotten better. He called me one night
years later when I was living in Cambridge to tell me that John Lennon
had been shot (we used to sit in one of his apartments getting high and

putting the needle down over and over on "Working Class Hero," imitating Lennon's nasal way of saying "fucking peasants . . ."), and I got from him that he was married and working as a high-end waiter (I could picture him that way, cleaned up, standing straight—he *was* a good-looking guy, with a Jack Nicholson smile he could turn on when he wanted). Another time, I got a picture in the mail—his daughter, born at about the same time my daughter, Mara, was born. He wrote then that he'd gotten a job as a maître'd at a classy restaurant and was making good money. No more painting, he added. That's where the thread breaks.

But even as I write this other images come back, scenes: the two of us hitchhiking through England in the summer of 1970, having a wild, ungoverned time, playing for days on end that we are characters from some movie he remembered. None of it made any sense, but we laughed and laughed, across England and over to Amsterdam, where he fell in with a hard-faced blond beauty named Aneeka and left with her on a train bound to India, and I went on to meet my friend Brad to travel to Spain. And one last thing. There was a thing he could do—for years—to get me going. It dates from that trip, and it's as senseless as anything else. Reddog would push his finger into his chin and dip his head and somehow fall perfectly into the voice and manner of Robert Mitchum. He knew he could always knock me over with that, no matter what sour business might be between us. After a while he didn't even have to do the act—he could just touch his chin with his finger. To me it was just as funny.

Plunge

That beautiful, up-to-the-elbows word *plunge,* all risk and gumption, caution waived, which is to say a moment of triumph over the sensible self—
who didn't dream it, or doesn't still? When I was young I was ready to
stake it all on a roll of the dice, so I thought. Whatever "it all" was, whatever I intended by "a roll of the dice." I don't think I had a clue. But I was
full of heroics. I had quotes tacked up around me: "No daring is fatal"—
this from a Frenchman named René Crevel. "I am trying to bribe you
with uncertainty, with danger, with defeat." That was Borges. I know
there was much inner ado about the leap, closing the eyes in a sudden access of trust. Like the party game of letting yourself fall, but without the
party. "The awful daring of a moment's surrender." T. S. Eliot, of course.
I kept myself busy, reading and copying quotes, putting them up over my
desks in the rooms I lived in. They were my prods. I hadn't even met up
with Kierkegaard, the master. "Purity of heart is to will one thing," he
wrote. When I found those words a few years later, little had changed. I
had neither advanced nor fallen back. I still went through my days with
the hope that something would pick me up and fling me over the preci-
pice as soon as I was worthy. Life would start, *now.* No, **now!** Wanting it
all so badly, no notion yet that the wanting was the thing—not for itself
but because the ache of *not enough* was the thread between words. Years,
cities, and now and again a real sentence. A run of sounds arriving from
someplace new. A pause: I see the reflection of my hand on the dark window over the desk. Daring, surrender. Tell what you know. *Find what
you know as you tell.* But who can teach it? I have my years of papers all
around me—in piles, in boxes. I feel I have neither advanced nor fallen
back, unless keeping on is itself advance, rather than evidence of futility.
No choice. Purity of heart is to will one thing. Plunge. Again.

"Blue Melody"

I'm kneeling on a mattress by the open window in your dorm room, Nina, and never mind that it was a hundred years ago, I can hear the bristly scratch of the needle on the turntable, and I feel the morning breeze coming in. Nina, Nina Taheri. Even now, all this time later, it's one of my favorite names to pronounce—those syllables melding so nicely. You were Iranian, though you said "Persian," and when we met you told me that your real name was Mina—even nicer! You were my girlfriend freshman year, a crazy time when it felt like everything was a story I was scribbling in my head. I was this, I was that. In one of my imaginings I was a hapless waif, and you were the dark-eyed—Persian-eyed—girl who recognized me and then took me in when I knocked. You had true kindness—or was it just that you couldn't say no to a man who so towered over you? I saw us paired up like Beauty and the Beast. My hair was long and brambly in those days, and you wore yours in a tight clasp. So many nights I would leave whatever chaos I was involved in—a dorm room party, some vast communal gathering down by the river—and start walking. Of course it was very late, but the time didn't matter: you would open your door and move over. There was the warmth of your spot in the bed, the smell of your hair . . . But this morning you must have gotten up to go to class and left me sleeping, because it's full daylight and I'm coming back to myself in pieces, going easy. I turn my head slowly to take in the things in your room, your little decorated boxes, clothes in a basket, textbooks, the one line of poetry you keep taped to your shelf. Roethke: "I have known the inexorable sadness of pencils." What on *earth* reached you about that line? Why did you copy it out and tape it there? I never got that. But never mind. Nina—you had that lovely down-turned mouth and slumped shoulder walk, and the tiniest breath of a mustache. Your real name was Mina June Taheri. Your father, I still know this, was a prominent doctor—a surgeon—in Bay City,

Michigan. I remember so little now of what you and I talked about, it's true. You had a shiny red plastic rain hat that brought your darkness out—dark eyes, black hair. And when you got stoned—which you did so rarely—the smile on your face turned almost crazy, I can't describe it. But I'm not all sieve. I do recall—and will still mumble, for no reason at all—your phrase, from the childhood game you told me about: nimi-nimi-nipi. That was the exact incantation, you confided it to me once like a secret. Nimi-nimi-nipi. What is it about memory? We had something between us. We talked and laughed and were not that often at a loss. And when I think of you first telling me the story of your game, saying those nonsense syllables, you are suddenly right here—your wide round face, tilting up at me, your mouth, your atmosphere . . . But what I'm remembering right now is your absence, the fact that I woke up this one morning and you weren't there. It was a spring day, one of the very first. I know, because the window was streaming in all this pent-up freshness. I felt it on my skin, and I was having one of those dizzy thoughts I used to get: that nothing had ever been like this before, not the day, or even the room with its pictures and books and the pasted-up line of Roethke's. I rolled off your mattress—we all slept in nests on the floor—and right away, before I did anything else, I started flipping through your milk-crate of albums and I picked Tim Buckley's *Blue Afternoon*. I get it all back. There was the familiar click and the rasp of the needle, and then the voice, I'm not sure I can describe it, and the utterly relaxed cadence of the strumming, the acoustic guitar blending with the vibes and the smooth, easy tone of Lee Underwood's electric guitar. I can still feel how that sound rose to meet the air, wrapping itself up with whatever was *in* the air, that sense I was having of life being freshened and moving forward. I got myself back over to the mattress, and I lifted my face up right into the window, and the vibes made a sound that hung there, like confetti. "If you hear a blue melody / won't you please send it home to me." I knelt like that through the whole long song, chin touching the window ledge, trying to get at the truth of all that sensation. What truth? The future, I suppose. Weren't we all dreaming the unimaginable next thing back then, and then it arrived—so soon—and kept arriving, each new wave of it slightly less unimaginable? "There ain't no wealth / That can buy my pride / There ain't no pain / that can cleanse my soul . . ." It was almost exactly forty years ago now—that gray spring morning in your tiny dormitory room, me listening to "Blue Melody" and waiting for you to come back from class.

Barcelona

I went to Barcelona in the summer of 1970, the great summer of European wandering, with cover stories in all the newsmagazines about a generation in search of itself, which is an irritating tag, a marketing hook, though I suppose it was also true. Of me, my friends, and all the people we met and mingled with in the hostels and on the beaches and in town squares, where we stretched out in groups near the fountains, resting against our backpacks, wetted bandannas tied around our necks, rolling cigarettes and exchanging tips about good places to sleep at night and free beaches. I was with my friend Brad at that point—we had met up in Brussels as planned and hitched our way down to Paris. Everything was an adventure that first day together—having no place to sleep, raving up and down all night along the banks of the Seine, keeping watch on the beautiful bridges, at one point stealing an unattended baguette from a parked car— "half for you, *mon frère,* and half for me"—leaning against each other on a bench as the sun came up, already hot, and deciding with exaggerated impulsiveness that Paris would be too hard to stay in, too expensive, and that we *had* to get to Spain immediately. Immediately, alas, meant finding how to get out of the city, its endless suburbs, meant walking with our big backpacks much of the morning, swearing at the trucks and the ill-mannered idiots who blew their horns as they tried to pick us off where we stood, thumbs out, so that we were completely spent, nearly in tears, before we took the first ride offered, from a man who was going not toward Spain, but to Aix-en-Provence. Who were we to argue? Aix-en-Provence is Cézanne, *n'est-ce pas?* It was the Mediterranean, or close enough. I can't patch together all of the stages now, though we worked them over into legend in the years to come.

There was a night in an open field, both of us gut-sick from whatever we had eaten at a roadside grille (was it *horse?*); and then an episode of panhandling, not in Aix but on the streets of Saint-Tropez, where we imagined we might charm the beautiful young Frenchwomen into giving us money, we were that full of ourselves—before we washed up a day or two later on an empty roadside near the Spanish border, so tired we were barely able to take our turns jumping up when we heard the sound of a car in the distance. It was a clear hot afternoon, I remember that, and we came to one of those moments—we had them every so often—when we looked at each other and announced a change in the flow of our luck. We both felt it, the shift, and this one time we had it right. A van with a hippie couple stopped, they were headed to Barcelona . . . I can't bring back the ride, the land outside the windows—we must have drowsed—only that it was dark and we were suddenly heaving our packs out the side door, saying good-bye to our kind drivers, looking to get our bearings on what we soon learned was the Rambla, the city's famous central boulevard. No more street wandering, we agreed, not that night. We had enough money between us for a cheap room, and the flow of our luck was still good—we found just such a place in a small hotel on a side street, where that first night we fell into our beds without undressing, with only enough energy between us to hit the light switch, and where the next night, this comes back like the memory of a vivid nightmare, I had my nineteen-year-old's version of a dark night of the soul, seeing more clearly than ever that I had no plan for my life, no idea what I might do or be. I sat up in my bed, my back against the headboard, staring at the magnified shadows of insects on the wall, with Brad not five feet away, reading a book, but at that moment too far away to call to, and what would I have said? But this was not what started me thinking about Barcelona. It was a movie Lynn and I watched on TV last night, most of which was set in that city. But the strange thing was that though I remarked on the fact—oh, yes, Barcelona—to myself when it started, I did it without feeling any connection to the place. I saw the streets, gardens, restaurants, Gaudí structures . . . I was much too caught up in the story, the convoluted romance, and had no thought of my own time there until a moment very late in the movie when two of the characters were shown standing in front of a great outdoor bank of cages, birdcages. Then all at once I had it, the sensation, like I was right there, back on the street with Brad that first morning. Rested, famished—I remembered—we'd hurried to get out

Barcelona
51

of our room, and of course we found our way down the little street right to the Rambla, which we'd hardly registered the night before. But now we started taking it in, the open lushness of it all, the blocks and blocks of flower stalls and fruits and jewelry, people everywhere, circulating, and then, abruptly, the area with the birds, birds of all descriptions, chirping and cheeping and tearing the air with their screeches, fluttering and shitting in their cages. But what came back, more than my amazement at all the sights, was the sudden feeling of freedom I had. It was as if I'd inhaled something. Not personal freedom—nothing tied to me—but something more general. I had the sense that inside this great city, this architecture of avenues and fine stone buildings stretching for blocks, was an impulse for flight, for getting up and away. Barcelona was like some vast air balloon surging against its tether. And as I walked farther I combined the sensation with the rest of the vista, for I found that as soon as I stepped away from the cages and flower stands and looked toward the end of the Rambla, everything opened onto the blue of the sea. The avenue was like a gateway, a runway. I was on my couch in the living room, but it all came back to me, required nothing more than those characters stopping there while the screen flashed the commotion of wings behind them.

Chessboard

This is a handsome, serious-looking chessboard, a kind of hinged wooden valise with squares on the outside and an embedded green felt space inside, with an elastic loop for each piece. Nothing decorative, though, no fancy character identities imposed on the pieces—they're just the standard shapes. The set says: let's have a real game. I gave it as a present to my son, Liam, years ago when it looked like he might have some interest in playing. For a few days it was his cherished possession. He carried it in both hands like a ring bearer's pillow and always set it down with great care. And then one day, when Liam was arranging the pieces on the dining room floor, Bumpers, the madly high-strung bichon frise that we had in what would prove to be very temporary custody, ran by, snatched one of the rooks, and engraved it all over with her sharp little teeth. That was it for Liam and his set. I don't mean that he wouldn't unpack it from time to time for a game, but from that moment on it lost its status as a cherished possession. I understand—I'm the same way.

To call chess a game is not really accurate. But it's how I thought of it when my father first taught me. I was young. I liked checkers and to me this was the same board, just a more complicated set of instructions. Also, I was intrigued, as any kid would be, by the ghost of a storybook narrative. Here was a king, a queen, knights, bishops, and a battlefield for them to go marching across. I learned the rules, and from time to time my father and I played. It is, I know now, entirely possible to view it as a simple contest, as a competition with prescribed moves, without ever getting immersed. I was still thinking that way a few years later when I sat down with Mr. Gulbis, my parents' Latvian friend, who came over specially to have a game. He was a great one for ritualized amusements. Whenever my parents went off on one of their trips and left my sister and me in the care of our grandmother, Mr. and Mrs. Gulbis would visit and we would all play canasta. I loved those nights.

But if canasta was sociable, chess was the opposite. When Mr. Gulbis—his Christian name was Ottomar—and I faced each other across the board we didn't speak. Time passed slowly; it took on mass. I would daydream while he studied the board, pushing back his long silver hair and every now and then dipping his index finger over one of his pieces but then pulling back again. I would get impatient. What could be taking so long? It all seemed plain enough to me—pick this square or that. But then he would laugh his low rumbly smoker's laugh and say, "I think the end is coming." This amazed me—because when he said that he was usually right. But how could he know what I was going to do? How could he look at the same pieces I was looking at and see into their future? I didn't understand chess yet. And then at one point a few years later, I did. I don't know what made the difference. I had not played much, if at all, in the interval. It must have been going up against my old friend Brad.

Brad and I got to be friends in my last year at Cranbrook, where he was my prod, my instigator, getting me out my window on school nights to go driving around the back streets of Detroit. Later he was my traveling mate—Mexico, France, Spain—and the two of us were never not nudging and testing each other. We were as close as blood brothers, able to talk the night away, but things were also complicated between us. When we grabbed each other and started wrestling—we did this every so often—things got bitterly serious right away.

The chess games would have come late in college. Brad and I were old friends by that time, but somehow we had never mentioned the game. Then one afternoon I was over at his place. He asked me if I played, and when I said I did, he started to smile. "Let's go," he said.

We drew for who got which color and then, still joking and baiting, set up the cheap plastic pieces. That was the last banter. As soon as the first pawn was played, I crossed a line—I went from playing a game with rules, a game of battle plans and decisions, to something very different. What happened? Instead of moving figures from the outside, from above, I woke up deep inside a contest of wills. By the middle of our very first game, I was completely overtaken. My mind had locked with his mind. It was as if we were maneuvering pieces in ways that stood for our own thinking; we were reading each other. In my mind's eye I lifted my knight to the space next to his bishop, and then I surveyed the whole of the game from the vantage of that choice. If he moved his rook, as he almost had to, then that pawn would be unattended. It was like that. I was not so much seeing the pieces as feeling their power and their potential, how they gained and lost advantage with every move. The array on the board, black and white, inert looking, was in fact crazy with energy, lines of it like bolts of lightning crisscrossing the sky. The two of us sat for hours in complete silence. We were faced off, and though I might have looked half-asleep, I was thinking as intensely as I had ever thought. Chess, I now understood, was absolute. No guesses, no accidents—this was not like the old days when I'd boldly skate my bishop along his open path. Now everything was weighed. I thought back to those long games with Mr. Gulbis. And I understood what people meant when they talked about the power of mind, how the good chess player can think so many moves ahead, while the master can double that.

Brad and I were pretty evenly matched. But whereas with most things we masked our rivalry, here it was in the open. We played for keeps and our games went for hours. Long Friday nights that started out loud with street sounds and then became strangely quiet. Cigarettes, wine. "What time is it?" We stayed at the board, sore eyed, in that place of pure combat. There were many face-offs. We played again and again because we came alive over chess.

That was all so long ago, and so simple. We were such antagonists, but beyond that we were friends, brothers. So I assumed. But I was wrong. For though the real-life pieces were pretty much all in place, I could not see ahead; neither of us could. There was no inkling of all the pain and betrayal that were coming. Chess was finally such a small part of how we knew each other. We had known each other for years, and now there were so many other things—other allegiances, our ambitions about writing, and the complexity of my old high school love, Beth. That had been a bitter trauma long ago, and Brad had been with me through much of it. It shouldn't have mattered any longer. I was well past it, with—and then no longer with—my great love, Sally, when Brad started seeing Beth. How did that all happen? Tellingly, I don't remember the details. What I know is that things between us were suddenly all different. "Between the motion / And the act / Falls the Shadow," wrote Eliot, and somehow that pertains; there was an edge, a feeling neither of us could name—it touched everything. I remember how we tried to joke past it for some time, but that didn't work. We even had an awkward dinner, the three of us, where Brad and I drank too much. Things were said and misunderstood and never fully repaired. Pride, rivalrousness—my old girlfriend Beth there at the end of the table, watching us. I still don't know what happened, just that the bad business grew until finally there came a day—I feel a wince all through me to remember it—when Brad and I passed each other in a restaurant in Ann Arbor without even nodding to each other. *Without even nodding.* We had reached a termination as absolute as the end of any of our games, except this time neither of us had the satisfaction of that last word: checkmate.

Cup

How is it that so many of our supposedly important artifacts end up keeping no charge of real meaning whatsoever while some incidental piece of ticky-tacky still glows like a marvel? I'm thinking right now of a cheap enameled tin cup, bright red, that I used for some years when I was just out of college and living in Ann Arbor. I don't remember how I came by it, just that I really liked the look of it—it seemed *writerly* to me. This was the time in my life when I saturated everything around me with the idea of writing, and the cup, one of the few things I owned in my minimalist existence, did not escape. I had it there next to me on the desk all the time I was working at my first stories. I would use my little hot-pot (to which almost no association has accrued) to boil water, and then stir up what I now think had to be an awful brew, adding two huge spoonfuls of freeze-dried Taster's Choice instant coffee, and then I would smoke and sip, wedged in there by the window with its blistered paint, its perforated screen, the smoke racing out with a fast upward suck. And though this same basic writing scenario could have taken place in a number of rooms I lived in—my desk was always pushed up near as possible to a window— I'm picturing right now the room I had above a delicatessen, situated at an especially loud intersection, where the grinding of the air conditioner mixed with the traffic noise, and all day long I inhaled the meaty stink from the back dumpster. That was when I sat at the desk window. The other window, where I had put the head of my bed, looked down onto the sidewalk in front, and I remember I would lie there on hot summer nights trying every trick I knew to get to sleep, my forehead crammed against the mesh, feeling off and on that uncanny sensation of levitating above the life of the street.

The red cup is the placeholder, the bookmark in what isn't a book, and I don't exaggerate when I say that thirty-some years later I can still see perfectly the burned-in, or crusted, irregularity at the bottom, that Rorschach blot I stared at when the last Taster's Choice was gone, while I sat and tried to be a writer. I had so little idea about how to get the words and phrases I wanted, even as I knew, or thought I knew, the sound I was after. That feeling of fumbling-after remains with me—I fumble every day—though the sound I want has changed a dozen times. Then I was doing a larcenous imitation of Julio Cortázar—"Julio," as I called him, following my tradition of familiar address of my heroes: Jack, Ernie, Knut, Henry, Blaise . . . Now I would say that the only person I want to sound like—and I pause to smile here—is myself. Can it be that our innocence is never entirely extinguished? I don't know how many hours I devoted to my various postures of creativity, and how few words finally got to the page. It was so much about the wanting, the getting ready, my having this idea that if the tip of the flame could find the end of the fuse some incredible explosion would result, blowing off the obstacle plate, with the words, sentences, paragraphs then all flooding out, confirming what I believed, that everything was really there the whole time, through all those undifferentiated spells of idling, when I twirled my pencil in my fingers and stared disconnectedly at the few things I had around me, at the spoon with its smudge of brown, the cutout magazine pictures pushpinned to the window frame, and of course the red cup that I knew would make a tinny little clang if I reached over to tap it.

Postcard

"Would I find La Maga? Most of the time it was just a case of my putting in an appearance, going along the Rue de Seine to the arch leading to the Quai de Conti, and I would see her slender form against the olive-ashen light which floats along the river as she crossed back and forth on the Pont des Arts, or leaned over the iron rail looking at the water."

There are sentences that change everything, like these—for me—from Julio Cortázar's *Hopscotch*.

I was a few months out of college and had gotten a job at Borders, the new bookshop that had just opened on State Street in Ann Arbor. I pinched myself all day long to make sure I was not dreaming. It was too good. After all those years of college, the classes that never fit right, even the good ones, all so far from what I longed for, which was a life of the mind that would wire me back to where I stood, or sat, that made sense when I looked out the windows of any of the rooms I lived in; after all the seasons of ill-paid drudge work—busing pizza trays, washing dishes, short-order cooking—I was finally home. I'd felt the rightness the first time I walked through the door into that long narrow space, before I even imagined I might apply to work there. The place was tailored just for me. I loved the look and the atmosphere: tall bookcases running the long length of the left wall, the best exposure given to fiction and poetry, new books interspersed with select, neatly hand-priced older books. There was no dross, no pandering to entertainment. I was susceptible, I admit, as romantic as could be in my daydreams. Sidestepping slowly along the wall—as I did day after day—or standing by the window table paging through the great gold-paper-covered volume of Jacques Henri Lartigue's photographs, I thought: *This—this is what I want!* Meaning not just the books but the promise created by all of them taken together—reading and writing, everything that four years of college had so completely skirted. And then one spring day, walking past the front register on my way out, I saw the posted notice about an opening for a clerk. Astonishing—how many corridors you walk through, turning this way, that way, trying different knobs, looking for entry, losing heart, before you come to the door that opens as if it were the easiest thing in the world and you just step through.

I worked at that store for a year, as happy as I've ever been, not once heaving the load-hoisting sigh of the day job. I was excited to arrive and start my shift, unpacking, shelving titles, arranging tables, packing returns, helping customers. My coworkers became friends. We were all readers, adding and subtracting from our employee stashes all day long. There was a writer—at least one—and a scholar of structuralism, soon off to Paris, a philosopher of the occult . . . We moved in close quarters and the air was charged. If anyone asked me what I did, I said that I wrote, or would someday. When the desire is that strong it almost counts for the deed, though in truth the only things I wrote were notes and convoluted reflections about the books I was piling up by my bedside and trying to read all at once. The madness of it—as if running in spurts in many directions gains one anything. Maybe it does. In any case, all that nightly sampling and cross-referencing was just another version of what went on all day long in the aisles of the store, shelving, perusing, being reminded of something, checking for that, making notes on a card I kept in my pocket: *koestler midwife toad* . . . and right below it: *saison en enfer.* These jottings and what they represent, over years and years of working in bookstores, and later just prowling—they are my education. And the path that leads to me typing here right now really did start there, that year after college, in those aisles and at those display tables. It was a new wanting, an appetite fired up by my coworkers and our customers, and the daylong jostle. Also the times, I can't forget that: ideas were sexy and authors were on the covers of magazines, and when a book like *Gravity's Rainbow* appeared, which it did while I was working there, we all felt a tremor move through our little world, if not the greater world that contained us.

I'd always been one for books and reading, but now I was truly combustible. In that season I passed from the state where everything seemed irresistibly interesting and felt the first thrill of narrowing: *not this book or this book but* this *book*. It was not all willy-nilly. One writer could take you to another, hand you off. There were tracks, courses of instruction, and which ones you followed would have everything to do with the life you made for yourself, or discovered waiting for you, that distinction being still negotiable. This was how I came to Julio Cortázar. I no longer remember what led to what—surely it was all intended—but there was the night when I bought from my stash the Plume trade paperback of a novel called *Hopscotch* and started reading: "Would I find La Maga? Most of the time . . ." Just as we mark big turnings in our outer life—new apartment, new job, travel—so we ought to mark these other shifts, the ones that happen as the tip of the finger is wetted and the page is turned. *Hopscotch*. What was it? The sound of the language, the bohemianism, the crazy experimentalism. Cortázar had structured the novel as a kind of assemblage—you could read it in any order, straight through or jumping. There was nothing like it anywhere. But for me the real draw was the attitude, the understanding, the philosophy behind it all. Here was a crazy, beautiful, and important book that verified everything I'd been toying with, all those ideas about coincidence and correspondences among things and people being destined for each other and fate tracing its phantom lines—there to be discerned, but only in the right light, only if you were looking. Cortázar had woven a whole grand novel out of it, and when I read it I became a believer. I went to the places he pointed out, looked for the writers he mentioned. I remember I copied a line from the novel and taped it up by my desk: "No daring is fatal"— attributed to the poet René Crevel.

Thus I proceeded, and proceeded. My life. And though many years have passed and much has happened, though I am strapped to the grid in ways I never foresaw, I can still sometimes catch a trace of the old fever when I look at a postcard I have taped to the wall not two feet from where I'm sitting. A head shot. Julio Cortázar in black and white. He is long haired, bearded, and pensive, his hand in front of his beard and his slightly bent index finger in front of his mouth. I fasten on the expression in the eyes, the gaze under his brows so completely severed from anything in this world. The man is thinking—thinking, I imagine, in the best, deepest way, where thought and feeling and remembered sensation fuse together so completely and compellingly that the gaze takes in nothing but the faintest outline of the outer scene. He is thinking as a writer thinks.

After a year of working at Borders I moved to Maine to undertake the writing life, and after two years, battered, I returned to Ann Arbor. During my absence Borders had relocated to a bigger space across the street, and the old location had become a shop selling used and rare books. As things fell out, I worked for a time as comanager of that store, filling those same bookcases with a completely different stock, carrying boxes of acquisitions up and down those old basement stairs. More changes: I abbreviate. After much inner struggle I left that job and moved East to try the writing life again. This time it stuck. Meanwhile, decades went by, during which time Tom and Louis Borders built their store into an empire, which they sold, and the shop in their original space, Charing Cross, went out of business. Living in Boston, caught up as I was in my new life, I followed these developments from a distance—which, as happens, widened and widened.

But then a few years back, out of the blue, I was invited to participate in a celebration honoring Karl Pohrt, a bookseller I had known all that time ago. I had not been to my old town in a long time. I was intrigued; I agreed. And then I flew in two hours across all that distance and sat in front of a room full of people and offered up my reminiscences about the Ann Arbor book scene in the 1970s. There was Karl, his brother, Tom, who had worked for a time in our shop, and people who came up later one after another to recall when they'd been customers.

It was one of life's moments of closure. And there was more closure to come. As I was leaving the room I ran into a woman I had once known very well. Sara. Sara had been the best friend of my old girlfriend Pam. What a grand surprise! How many years? Of course we started right in, edging away slowly from the people in the room, until we finally decided we had to go have lunch together. Sara had time, I had time. We made our way slowly down State Street, saying "here?" and "how's this?" before finally stepping into something called, I think, the Red Hawk Grille. I should have noticed, really, but we were talking, talking in the best familiar way, which meant not really registering anything else. We were seated. I checked out the menu and ordered. And ate. And even then I was still oblivious, which I now think was maybe not so strange since absolutely everything was different, rearranged, with a huge long bar up along the right-hand wall, marked-off areas for tables and booths elsewhere. No, it was only at the end, after I excused myself to use the bathroom and pushed through a doorway, when I was at least halfway down the stairs, that I got it. The news reached my body first—something was familiar here, the width between walls, the height of the steps, the way my legs took them, the molecules of dust gathered in that dim well. I stopped. *Oh my God!* It was all at once so striking to me, striking in that Cortázar way, where you know something momentous has happened but you also know you'll never be able to say how or to what end. I stood there, pulverized. Pulverized and rearranged. When I returned to the table a few minutes later I told Sara, knowing she would get it, too. And she did. She knew this place, of course, what it meant. But there was nothing more either of us could do with it. We shook our heads and smiled and then looked at each other the way you do when you are greeting the uncanny absolute.

Finding the Level

Steven Tyler. I think that was actually the guy's real name, though I know I won't ever get it back for sure now that there's the other musician, the Aerosmith singer, Steve Tyler, in my head. And if it was in fact something else, it doesn't matter—except insofar as I pride myself on keeping certain long-gone names vivid even as I fumble and miss with every third student in whatever class I'm teaching. Steven Tyler. I thought of him today while driving along the MassPike on the way to visit Mara at Hampshire College, making the drive that I used to make twice a week without fail for six years when I taught at Mount Holyoke, and falling I'm sure into some ancient prescribed groove of reverie. I don't believe I had my old days in Maine in mind, though that's where the memory fits, and I don't even know that I was thinking about guitar playing, not directly, anyway, though I was listening to a blues-mix CD that a former student's father had made for me, and of course that could have started me in that direction. In any case, the point of the story is less about music itself than it is about having one of those experiences that lets you know you've stepped completely out of your depth. I suppose I should ask myself why this is coming up just now.

Steven Tyler. This was the mid-1970s in Maine. I was living in Biddeford Pool with Sally, both of us scratching hard for a living. The feeling is readily summoned. Sally was just starting to sell the occasional watercolor on consignment at a gallery in Kennebunkport, and I had gotten a part-time job working in the so-called College Relations Office at what was then Saint Francis College, going in every day half-time to spin ideas with my boss, Dave DeTurk, and to follow up with whatever legwork was needed to write the necessary story or press release. Dave, whom I enjoyed so much, my first "hip" boss, was the coauthor of *The American Folk Scene,* a book I'd picked up before I actually met him. He was a thin, nearly chain-smoking—back when people still chain-smoked—enthusiast, a cleaned-up beatnik, radically out of place at the college, though probably less so than I was. When we originally met in the hallway, I was weeks into my original job for the college—I was working as a night janitor. We got to talking and must have talked long enough for him to realize that I had been to college and read books (no mention of folk music then). I felt something click between us. And when a few weeks later he found a way to get a bit of funding for an assistant, he offered the job to me. It was a very big lift for us on the home front. The money problem did not go away, but for a time our scrambling at least had some more net under it.

I haven't thought of Dave in a long time, but—this is odd—last month while I was in Indiana giving a talk I mentioned him to one of my hosts. For his coauthor on the folk book had been the poet A. Poulin Jr., whose name had come up in our lunchtime conversation, and I was able to announce, as I otherwise never can, that I had once lived in the same apartment Poulin had lived in (which was true—at Winter Harbor Apartments in Biddeford Pool). And that I had worked for his then coauthor Dave DeTurk. And though no one at the table had any interest in that last bit of information, I felt very happy to offer it. As for the musician, Steven Tyler, that connection came about through someone at the college. Dave had set me up to interview the director of the school radio station, which I did, and after the interview, chatting, I mentioned in some context that I played the guitar. Possibly—probably—I exaggerated my level as a player. In any event, this radio person started telling me that there was a fabulous guitar player living just down the road from the college, a guy who had once played with all the famous bands but who had run into some hard times and was now "retired." I should look him up, he said. Maybe we could play together. Steven Tyler. He gave me the number.

Of course I thought this was providential, a sign from the heavens that I should, indeed, follow up. I was young and our life was spare and quiet. I would not act so impulsively nowadays. But nowadays there are people everywhere in my life, and back then, Sally aside and Dave aside, there was no one at all. So I can be excused for imagining a whole new life unfolding as Steven Tyler and I establish musical rapport and he introduces me to his vast network of musician friends. I made the call. I punched the numbers—my heart, I'm sure, pounding in my chest—and he answered right away. What's more, he seemed interested enough. He said, "Sure, let's get together." He told me where he lived—it *was* right near the college—and we made a date for me to stop by the next day.

Oddly, I don't remember anything about getting to his house, though I would have had to have gone on foot, since I remember quite clearly walking the long way home, shifting my case from hand to hand. One moment I was on the phone, noting down his address, and then I was there, knocking, and a tall, long-haired, shambly looking guy in jeans and a T-shirt was inviting me in. He had a comfortable but run-down house (I do remember this), a large open-looking living room, almost no furniture at all. There was his guitar in a big serious-looking case in the corner. Me? Well, I was clutching my original old small Gibson in its amateur-looking case. I set it down, looked around. He offered me a seat at the kitchen table. I think we smoked (I'm sure I did), and we talked. He was—I took this in with a slight jolt—probably ten years older than I. I don't know what I'd expected, but I might have gotten the first hint then that I was in over my head. Tyler offered me coffee. He asked me what kind of guitar I had ("It's a B-25 Natural," I said) and was—I see now—polite enough not to laugh in my face. I asked him the same, though my knowledge of guitars was nonexistent. I don't remember what he told me. He asked what kind of music I played. I probably didn't say "Freight Train" and "Candy Man"— the truth. Likely I shrugged and said, "Blues, folk . . ."

Was it at this point I started wishing I could dematerialize and walk through walls? I asked him the same question back. He told me—I still see the look on his angular, haggard-looking face—that he had worked with a lot of musicians before things got complicated and he had to take a break. I asked who. He named some names, all bands that I'd heard of. Then he said that he had jammed with Jimmy Page once. And Keith Richards. He shook his head in a way that said it all. I felt my stomach go sour. Keith Richards. Jimmy Page. Suddenly there was only the question of how I would get out of the room and down the road. But no, there was a stretch of time to be gotten through. We had our coffee. There was no beer, no wine—this was obviously part of the story. We talked more—God knows what about. Until at one point there was nothing to do but take the next step. He asked if I wanted to take out my guitar and play something. I must have nodded. What was I hoping for—that the patron god of self-important young men would take pity on me and touch my fingers with lightning? It was right then, before I even leaned over to unsnap my case, that I understood with perfect objectivity how good I really was. By which I mean that I was not good at all, not even in hailing distance. Whatever fantasies I deluded myself with when I was sitting up in our place drinking my cups of merlot and strumming, here was the truth: I was a ground-floor beginner, a guy with about three licks and no essential command of music. I had my labored fingerpicking versions of a handful of songs, a few notes I could bend when I was inspired. And I was about to humiliate myself in front of a musician who had played with Jimmy Page. What did I do? I sucked in a breath and marched right on. I took out my little Gibson B-25 Natural and pretended to tune it, while Tyler maybe noted, "a bit sharp on the B," or something like that. And then I cannonballed my way through whatever song I had that was closest to blues. After a few bars I stopped. I couldn't do it. There was a moment of terrible silence. I winced. But the man saved me. He nodded and said, "That's some good stuff to work on." What better words could he have found? And I nodded and laughed and said yeah, that I knew I needed to practice more. And he laughed, too, easier now, and said, "Gotta start somewhere, man." I didn't stay long after that. I packed up my guitar, we shook hands, I thanked him for the coffee, and I started off in the dark down that long road that ran along the edge of the great tidal pool, a good three-mile walk to our place, shifting my case hand to hand, over and over picturing his case there by the wall, never even opened, wishing in spite of my pride that I could have heard what a guy who had jammed with Jimmy Page and Keith Richards sounded like.

Ladder

It was already there when I came around the side of the house. I saw it in that sidelong way you register one thing while looking for another. I was trying to find the man I'd spoken to on the phone, who had hired me for the day, and there he was, cross-legged on the grass, wearing a bright white T-shirt, with a full head of silvery hair, camera hair, though he didn't really look like the kind of older man who would go to all the trouble. But maybe he was, because when he heard me coming and turned full-face I saw he was handsome, lady-killer handsome the way some older men are, and these men are always vain. He was cleaning paintbrushes— they were neatly lined up on a sheet of newspaper—and he didn't get up. He had strong-looking arms, maybe even an old-style tattoo. I was look- ing, staring, at his face, but not so distracted that I didn't take in the other thing. Off to my right, propped up against the side of the house, going up and up in sections, was the tallest ladder I'd ever seen. I felt a bump in my stomach. I hadn't even really turned yet, or followed the ladder up into the light to see where the ends were propped against the highest gable. I was still making my way across the grass, and the man, I don't remember his name anymore, was squinting up and saluting me, or maybe lifting his arm to block the sun, saying, "Here to do some work?" I nodded and said I was. That was the deal. I'd been living on the edge all winter in our little seaside Maine town, buying dented canned goods at discount and even signing on one day with my girlfriend, Sally, to deliver phone books in nearby Biddeford, the mill town in which every other person was named Pelletier or Thibodeaux—and we were required to check off the right re- cipient and address. Thibodeaux, Thibodeaux, Thibodeaux . . . We quit after a day. Next I'd put up a sign in our little cracker-box post office of- fering my odd-job services for a laughably low hourly rate. My logic: who could resist?

And now it was one of the first real spring days and this man had called with a job, and my attention was evenly split between the shock of his seasoned movie-star looks and my growing awareness of that ladder. Did I already know how it was with me and heights? How could I not? I was in my early twenties and had done enough playing in trees and high places as a kid to have an idea. I'd always been a reluctant climber, though maybe I'd later chalked it off as a fear outgrown—as if a decade of not testing the edge would have made it go away. I don't know. I only know that the man—my boss—walked me over to where the ladder stood flat on its grips and showed me my bucket and brushes and handed me a rag that I tucked into my belt. But just before he did that—this comes back with close-up clarity—he reached his thumb and forefinger into the two corners of his mouth and took out his teeth. Out. The whole apparatus. He pulled it from his mouth and held it up like one of those party jokes that you wind with a key. I looked away—I felt embarrassed—and when I glanced back I must have done a double take. Impossible. His face had completely fallen in on itself—the strong jaw was gone, the mouth was crimped like the top of a string bag. I watched as he bent down and set the teeth on another sheet of newspaper in the grass.

When he straightened up, I was face-to-face with an old man with a thick, groomed head of silver hair. I don't know if he had any idea of the effect he had just achieved. He was standing with me by the ladder, telling me to make sure I got enough paint onto the wood, and I was nodding, agreeing, and already registering—I'm sure of it—that first nervous heaviness in my legs, and that tightness in the chest that starts you drawing deep breaths as if a good deep rush of air will make everything better. And then I was on the ladder, starting, a few rungs up, hauling the bucket with my left hand, the shore in sight, the ground still an easy jump. I had that instinct, or instruction, picked up somewhere, to keep my gaze straight ahead, taking in the lapping shingles row by row, the voice that said, "Don't look, just climb." Which I did, so carefully, every bit of my focus on my legs and hands, and on keeping the line of the vertical steady—no twists or turns, just plant the foot on the rung and pull with my one free arm, the right arm, the other gripping the bucket, which I was to hang on a hook next to where I painted—and I was already telling myself the facts of the matter, that people did this all the time, everywhere; that the ladder was strong, well planted at the base; and that little wobbles would naturally be magnified as sensations, that there was no real danger, and that even if I were to fall—*I would not fall*—it would be nothing more than a bad bump and some embarrassment at this point. So I stepped and pulled and steadied and watched myself in slow blurry sections pass by the frame of the first big window, which I knew was about halfway up.

But here the ordinary sequence stops. This upward progress was not happening in units anymore, never mind the rungs lined up ahead of me. Somewhere between one step and another the time stream balked, then stopped and started backing up. Every movement was suddenly breaking into its parts, the one arm aware of itself lifting, wrapping its fingers around the metal of the next rung, the other hand feeling in its joints the cut of the handle, the weight of the bucket, the weathered shingles mere inches away now gathering into the clearest detail: nail heads, streaks and smears and hardened little droplets of ancient paint, the ribbing of the wood grain visible under the color. "Don't look down, just climb." And I could feel it then, on my skin, up the armholes, the April wind, sweetly cool even in the spots of full sun, which I knew without looking was moving in and out behind the clouds. The moment of the shift. It comes now. I hear myself breathing and realize that I've stopped. I don't remember stopping, but all at once I know that I've been staring and staring at the same few warps and scratches. How long? I don't know. The window below me rattles in the breeze, I hear it. Suddenly I can't help myself: I turn my head just slightly to the left and I look down. Mainly to see if the man, my boss, is still there somewhere, but also because I need to know where I am. I feel a kind of thud as the scene clicks in. Ground, grass. He's not anywhere on the left side. Nor—I've moved my head so carefully, as if that little action could make a difference—on the other. The lawn falls away in either direction, empty. I am halfway up the side of the tallest house I've ever seen and I'm alone. And that little twist of the neck was like breaking the seal. The calm, the focus, whatever story I was telling myself up here, is gone. I take in the great wide lawn, and over there, tiny as a kit for dolls, the newspaper with its row of tiny brushes lined up, and one corner flipping up in the breeze. That repeating movement makes me feel sick, that and the ground all at once so far away, the wind now pulling at the back of my shirt, and I feel the fingers of my right hand tighten their grasp and my chest and stomach push in harder against the rungs. What have I done? I can't unsee the distance down, or lose the sense of the ladder shrinking away to nothing below me and above me. My hand hurts where I hold the metal, and now my knees go soft, just like that. I have the weight of the bucket in my other hand. For the first time I think, *Let it go, just drop it*—drop it and reach up with that hand, as if maybe with both hands gripping I can make it down. But somehow I can't make myself loosen my hold on the bucket, or do anything. Except close my eyes. Close my eyes and start to count, slowly: *One thousand one, one thousand two . . .* I don't know how high I get, but after enough numbers I feel something in me settle, I say to myself, *OK now,* and as I say that I get my fingers to go loose, and then without ever taking them away from the ladder I slide them, along the rung to the right-hand side, and then down the metal slowly, clutching between thumb and forefinger, until I reach the nearer rung, which I grab, and as I do that I let my left leg loose to find the lower support, and this I find, and lower the other leg, foot, shuddering my torso inch by inch down along the rungs, and again repeating the whole sequence, gaining just the first slight ease as the ground lifts slightly toward me, again, again, until I reach the first rung and take the backward step to earth, almost crazy with reaching it, bending to set the bucket down, letting go my other grip and straightening slowly up . . . and only then becoming aware of the man standing right in back of me. He's arrived from somewhere, and I know he's seen the whole of it, and at the same time I can feel that the fingers of my left hand, free from the clutch and the weight, are shaking. But I have no doubt, no question. Standing there, I notice where the shadows—mine, his—break from the grass against the side of the house, and I say to him without turning around, "I can't go up that high. I didn't know it before." I wait for a moment. When I finally turn and meet his eye, he shrugs, saying basically, *What can you do?* He's wearing a painter's cap now, flecked with white paint, and I see that he has put the teeth back in—and he looks good, not quite Paul Newman, but very handsome. Obviously a lady-killer.

Tomcat

In 1977 I was living in Ann Arbor, sharing an apartment with my then girlfriend Pam, a third-story space shaded by tall trees, with an old-style wooden fire escape that came right up to our large kitchen window to create a kind of deck. We used it for that, keeping the window open all summer, moving in and out to sit on the edge of the platform, having our coffee there in the morning, beers at night. The summer, I remember, was long and hot and we were always out there, trying to catch whatever breezes we could, and enjoying the light like two Icelanders, because the rest of the place was so dark and atticlike. I was working at Charing Cross Book Shop then, dealing used and rare books all day long with my partner George, and resolutions about restraint notwithstanding, I came home every night with more books. They filled the far wall of our little bedroom, spilling over into stacks in every corner. I could see that this was becoming a problem, but I didn't stop coming home with bags. Truth is, I like the feel of a place that is overrun with books. I remember how I used to lie on my back in bed and let my gaze bump slowly and methodically from spine to spine, looking away every so often to renew my contract with what I believed was my true vocation—writing. The idea then was that I was dealing books just to make money; I was building up steam for making a break. Soon enough I knew I would explode into a new life, make good on my promises, typing like a man possessed, filling pages, sending to magazines. But just not yet. I wasn't quite ready to give up the life I had going. I still enjoyed getting my morning coffee at Kresge's and then crossing the street to unlock the store; I liked planning the day's buys, sorting through new purchases with George, and joking around with the regulars. And if one of them asked me how my writing was going, I would find a way to deflect, managing to suggest that great things were in the works without ever saying what those might be. And so the season went on, the long summer, window open to the light, Pam and I pursuing our own jobs and friends throughout the day, connecting up at night, to cook and drink beer on the fire escape. Sometimes—pretty often, it seems now when I look back—I was by myself in the apartment, sitting on the edge of the bed in the slope-ceiling bedroom near my bookshelves, scheming my life while I tilted my head slowly this way and that.

I was in that posture when I first saw it. Something. A large yellow blur in my peripheral vision. When I creaked on the bedsprings there was a rush, a fast reverse scuttle. I got to the kitchen just in time to see the swerve of a thick tail and then hear a light thud as it landed on the fire escape. When I got to the window it had vanished. A cat, obviously one of the toms we always heard yowling at night down by the garbage cans.

I don't like cats, I never have. I think of them as cold and sneaky, two attributes that my wife, Lynn, a therapist, insists are pure projections on my part. I know without being told that this doesn't reflect well on me, but there it is. My response to seeing the yellow tom in our apartment was to become hypervigilant. I didn't, as someone else might have, just close the window. Not only was it too hot, but that would have been a gesture of defeat; I would be allowing an alley cat to dictate to me. No, I left the window open and went back to my spot. But from that time on I stayed alert. I had no choice. I didn't *want* to think about the cat, but I couldn't stop myself. In fact, the more I tried to forget that blurry shape, the more it cut into my focus.

In the next days there were other episodes, bolder visits. Once I came out of the bathroom and found the creature standing at full attention in the middle of the living room. He looked at me and read my mind, and with a bunching of the back and a few quick muscular leaps he was up onto our breakfast table and out. I realized I was breathing heavily, as if I had just climbed the stairs. Then a few days later I walked in the room and found him hovering right in the window, tilted forward, right at the point of jumping in. With a flash of tail he was gone.

Now he seemed to be coming daily. And still I couldn't make myself close the window, not when I was home, even though he was taking up more and more of my attention. Then I got my idea. It was beautifully simple—and obvious. First I got a long piece of string and tied it to the window latch so that I could yank it shut from the other room with a single pull. Next I filled a washbasin with cold water and put it near the kitchen door. And then I waited. And waited, and waited. Like a fool. Aware of myself as a fool. But I didn't care. I kept on with it, that day, and then the next.

I'm struck now by the fact that Pam had no part in any of this drama. Where was she? Was she working or studying? I can't remember. Nor can I say why I was there so often. What was going on with my job? Where was I getting these free afternoons? Work didn't usually end until after six. How was I able to be there all those days in that hot little bedroom space, waiting? But I was, in memory anyway. And the being there, the waiting, paid off. Because right in the dead center of a hot summer afternoon I looked up and saw him there. Just like that. Tense, rigid, only a few feet away, staring at me, me staring back, as if we'd been doing this all our lives, the tom not moving so long as I was still, every muscle on alert, staying like that even as I edged my hand a few inches over, leaping only in the same wild instant I yanked the line, but not quickly or powerfully enough, for as I then got to my feet I saw he was there, bunched up next to the stove, slightly bigger suddenly, as if he'd grown in those few seconds, watching me again, poised as I made my way toward the basin, but then whirling into fast motion as soon as I ducked, so he was now in the living room, beside the couch, in the corner, with nowhere to go but up and over. I picked up the bucket with both hands, my breath tied in big hard knots in my throat. I felt more awake than I had for months. And then—I picture it now like the famous surrealist photo, the one with Salvador Dalí and the flying cats—the water fanned out flat in a quicksilver shape, clear to the last stray droplet, pure chaos immobilized. Here were the two of us, the tom and I, in the slow time of assassination and calamity, the whole bucket of water hitting him broadside, his raspy primal screech like nothing I've heard, his incredible leap free of the couch and room and gravity-bound frame of one of his lives a sure world record, followed in the very same second by the crash of his big body against the window frame, and then the giving creak of the hinge and the multiple thumps of his amazing getaway. There is nothing more to be said. The wall and carpet were soaked, but they would dry. I knew that the yellow cat would never come back. I stood by the window and glowed for a while with the satisfying shame of my violence. Over and done. It wasn't really until this morning, when I remembered the whole business, that I saw how it was another story, too, a kind of literary self-portrait, though I would have to think about how to tell it so that the cat in that corner was not too obviously me in my life, my every muscle flexed for flight.

Apple

I stopped myself this afternoon. I did that thing I sometimes need to do: I stood by the glass door to the deck and said, "Look." And then, "No— *look!*" Don't just see what you see every time you walk past, skimming the eyes over what you remember or believe to be there. But look. There: at the tree, the apple tree, with its horse-collar hollow all dug out by squirrels and its peeled-off bark, the old snapped-off branches and their quivers of straight reedy suckers. And the green garden ladder, found I don't remember where, that I leaned up against the trunk last fall, not as an aesthetic gesture—God forbid!—but because I noticed it in the bushes by the side of the house, and I thought it would make a silly little narrative—as if there were apple picking to be done, or we had children who might still want to play. But there are no more apples, the last few went to brown paste under my rake years ago, or squelched away on my shoes when I walked over them carrying leaves. And the kids—if they ever climbed the ladder now it would be ironically, mugging the idea of childhood to a visiting friend or each other. Still, it's the ladder that catches me. I slip in an instant from the blighted fright of the tree—its beauty that of a broken thing—to that innocent leaning shape, and then all the way back. To the fall we bought the house, nineteen years ago, and there was the malt of apple in the air, and things seemed rich and simple, almost rural. We had the big Glenwood stove in the kitchen, with logs for burning stacked up under the porch, and I loved the way those hanging apples filled the air, hovering over the deck, thunking hollow on the boards through the night. Our first season of occupancy was for me about that sound, and the afternoon vibration of bees, drowsing over the sap, and the smell coming in through the upstairs window for days on end—and then one cold morning the startling bare-wire look of branches. For years and years that apple tree was its own performance, tracing the ancient cycle, the apples coming late in summer and the spectacular flourish of pink white in early spring, the buds always opening in the night, there like applause in the morning light, then an encore that lasted for days. Was anything finer than all that color crowding in? I don't think I ever wondered where the tree came from. For me it was just *there,* making its fruit. It was only years after we moved in—the kids were long since lords of the yard and the street—that I got the story. An old man who was doing some work for us, painting—his name was Mr. Finochetti—took his break and got me talking. We were out back, on the deck. "This—" he said, motioning out over the rail at the neighborhood. "All this—you wouldn't believe it. When I was a kid this was all orchards. This here was one of the few houses. This apple tree"—we both looked up—"well, this area was *all* fruit trees." He said more, he said it better, and with every sweep of his hand, in his every pause, I felt familiar things get deeper. I took it all in. That this long roll of land now cluttered with houses and yards had all been orchard—this old tree just one of many—I tried for a picture, a scramble of ladders and hands and baskets. And with Mr. Finochetti standing there it came real, and the feeling held—the world unwritten, rewritten, suspended in front of me—until after another long moment, it faded, the yards and houses pushing back, the cars moving up and down the street. Now? Now it's barely a ghost story, a memory of an imagining, a strange sensation that will sometimes reach me when I come downstairs in the first light, but nothing more. The tree itself survives, wild and scraggly, parked up full of messy nests, but all vestige of the glowing, yielding thing is long gone. Once in a great while, though, I will stand out on the deck on a warm fall night, an arm's reach from what remains, and I will get the faintest tang of that sour gone liquor, that trashy exhilarating reek, intimate as the hand reaching down the body or the afterbreath of love.

It

And how is it that *it* comes to have a place of such honor—the open top shelf of the living room bookcase, that otherwise tightly packed tartan of spines interrupted only here and there by a special photograph in a frame? I'll tell you. Oddness, beauty, and mystery—those are the criteria I come up with, but only after the fact, when I ask myself why I can neither get rid of this thing nor demote it. I don't mean this to be a guessing game. *It* is a lightbulb. And if I didn't identify it as such right away it's only because I don't want to sell the wrong image. Because it's not like any bulb I've ever see before. It's an ocean bulb, a sea light, I don't know. We found it washed up on the sand on a beach on Martha's Vineyard many summers ago, the point here being that origins not only offer no clue, they also enhance the mystery. I'm sure I would regard my bulb differently if it had turned up in an alley behind an old foundry or was picked up as part of an odd lot on a yard sale table. No, the idea of ocean, ships, and distances suffuses it, as does some vestigial folkloric notion of a message in a bottle. Though not a bottle, it is bottle-*ish*.

Some description is wanted. This object, this "lightbulb," is the size of a small eggplant, fashioned from clear glass, clear *thick* glass. The top, however, is not rounded like the top of a regular household lightbulb, but indented, a pinkie-sized nipple shape protruding in toward the interior. The opposite end has a wide copper bulb-screw, with the insertion ridge (of course that's not the name) coiling down five rotations to the crusted-over contact element. None of this is especially interesting. What compels the eye, and accounts, to me, for much of the beauty element—and the oddness—is the highly elaborate interior architecture. No simple filament this. It's a Rube Goldberg contraption standing in the stead of a ship in a bottle, and the eye does not tire of contemplating. From the bottom, projecting from the contact at the base, is a tawny little turret, big as an earplug, but glazed and shiny, from which protrudes a small two-pronged device. Each prong is connected to a fine metal strut, and these are then connected by a thin perpendicular bar. Above the bar, pinched by it as by a bobby pin, is one end of what looks like a thumb-sized glass vial with a flattened top and bottom. The vial is about two inches long, and its other flattened end is clasped by another metal crosspiece, this joined to another metal strut, the top end of which hooks onto a metal circlet that girds the nippled indentation. Got that? I'll stop. I've only traced the main artery of the thing—there are minute wires and clasps and spring and spindle components on both sides of the vial and its support system. But description gets tiresome. And it is also misleading, for nothing I have written here gives even a hint of the beauty of the thing. Maybe because the beauty is not found in the parts or their elaboration, but rather in the overall effect: so much orchestrated metal, such a map of causality—I think of those shortwave radio kits I used to stare at in the crafts store, unable to fathom what kind of brains it would take to get one up and running. This bulb has so much mysterious purpose packed inside its smooth glass. The transparency is almost a kind of optical privilege, like those clear plastic bodies we were supposed to fill with colored organs—"The Visible Man"—that kit also on display in another aisle of the same crafts store. Only here transparency is not a trick, it's the point. This is a lightbulb, and all the business inside is for the making of light, illumination. No glass, no point.

But what was it doing on the beach? What fathoms did it go bobbing through, and why, to end up there on the sand to be scavenged by us? By itself it was one string end of a story—pull with enough imagination and you might find what the other end is tied to. Or maybe not. The beach is strewn with these string ends. In some cases literally. For it was on the same stretch, that same summer, that I came upon a genuinely satisfying length of rope, and it really was with the end that I began. This was something out of *Robinson Crusoe,* half buried, thick as a thick garden hose, about which you would say, as I'm sure I said a hundred times, later, "This is a *rope.*" A rope as a made thing, a piece of property, a good strong ten yards of it meandering along the sand, no way not to take it back, first to the house where we were staying, but then, later, back home. I remember coiling it around hand and bent elbow, over and over, taking in the real weight of it, and then hefting it up, aloft, as I crossed the inlet, or basin, that separated the beach from the house we were renting. And of course I stared down as I slogged knee-deep across, because this water was teeming—*teeming*—with blue-green crabs. They were everywhere, scattering like the armies of the Saracens before the righteous Crusaders, and it was then, or very soon after, that I got my big idea. Risotto. Crabmeat risotto, made with crabs that my son, Liam, and I would net. That was what I called a plan. But first the kid had to see this rope. What boy, what male of the species, would not go mad with dreams when presented with such an item? And he did. Or did he? I'm not sure. He was only eight or nine. He hadn't read *Crusoe* or *The Swiss Family Robinson*. Maybe he stretched it out on the grass in front of the house and kicked it and then lost interest. I would have wound it up again and put it by the door so as not to forget to take it home.

But Liam did agree to hunt crabs with me, this I know. And we had a good hour of it with our little nets, filling a bucket. He happily scooped for them, whooping and thrashing while also monitoring the sand by his feet, but I had to prod them loose from the mesh—he didn't like doing that. Still, he was as proud as I was of the booty we amassed—the bucket was jigsawed with the creatures. Unfortunately, he was not nearly as interested as I'd hoped in the rest of the business: boiling, or helping to pry the meat from the shells and stir it into the risotto. Nor did he, this I also know, partake of the repast, which truth be told was not such a repast. I dished it out to Lynn and myself. Mara and Liam ate chicken nuggets. We dipped our forks. Lynn straightaway pronounced the meat "tough," and after disagreeing for a time I agreed. Much of what was left got dumped into the garbage bag with those beautiful green-blue shells, which a neighbor happened to tell me the next day belonged to an ecologically fragile species that was just beginning to "come back" in certain inlet areas on the Vineyard. I said nothing. Our bag was tied and hidden deep in the trash barrel. The vacation ended. The rope and the bulb were packed in the back of the car. As soon as we got home to Arlington I climbed the ladder we keep propped against our moribund apple tree. I tied one end of the rope to a branch and put a big knot in the other: every childhood should have a thick swinging rope somewhere in it. The bulb, as I said, perches on the top shelf of the living room bookcase, and when I'm done with perusing my spines left to right to left to right, I sometimes let my gaze rest on that vexing little artifact. What the hell is it? Why all that gimmickry inside? To understand why it looks like that I would have to know what it screwed into, what it was meant to light.

Lighter

Found things and the stir they make in memory—that's one ecology. But there's another, no less important, that describes the shadow world: all the things we simply lose, or lose and then, on finding, find without spark. As if to say we are as much about our deletions as our accumulations. Yesterday I came home from a short trip to find a belated Christmas present in my mail, a bulky soft bundle from my brother, Erik. It was a thick fleecy sweatshirt he had special-ordered, embossed with my (and his) old high school insignia. But wait—something else! There was also a small, tightly wrapped packet tucked in, and with it a note from Erik. "Something I found in my last sweep through the old place," he had written. He was referring to the visit he and his wife, Alison, had made to see my parents right before they sold the house and moved East. I palmed and hefted the packet, mystified—and then slowly worked the tape loose. The paper-covered weight in the hand disclosed a dull silver sheen. A cigarette lighter. *Ah* . . . I felt the quick flash of wires making first contact. *The lighter!* But then right away came the pause. Wait, where did he get *that?* Hadn't I destroyed it—the relic, my father's old prize from the war? There was an afternoon maybe fifty years back, me alone in the house doing my irresistible demolition, working loose the parts, the little screws and cylinders and laying the whole thing out for study on his drafting table. And then there was the scene later, when my father came home from the office. There was— But no, this couldn't be right. How could Erik have known about that? Had I written about it? Well, yes, I had—but barely, in passing. I doubted he would have read it, or, having read it, would possibly have remembered. Still, I got a faint waft of conjectural self-flattery: my brother reads *me!* But then suspicion came chasing after: If he *had* read it, had remembered, then this was a joke, a little brotherly dig. A wink. But a wink meaning what? Standing there by the counter, I couldn't help but consider the speed of supposition: this whole scenario of second-guessing unfolded so quickly. I'd just a moment before lifted the thing from its wrapping and now I was holding it up between thumb and forefinger, inspecting, and for some reason I looked at the bottom first. There I saw a hole, a place for a missing screw. Maybe it *had* been reassembled, redeemed. And though I knew that if I flicked the lighter bar nothing would happen, I did—once, twice, again, each time imagining the clean leaf of a blaze. Then I gave it another turn in my fingers, another tilt of the wrist, and when I did this the whole investigation fizzled. There, plain as could be on the flat side: S P B. My engraved initials. The lighter had been mine. Mine! Clearly once a gift given, received, and put to use. For of course I would have put it to use. But now, in the wake of all that first surmising, I get no picture. Just a blank the size of the lighter, and those three initials like the bread crumbs that the woodland birds had gobbled down. No way back for me. I stare at the thing, waiting for some small pulse of recollection, some *Of course!* But there is no glimmer right then and no feeling that anything might be en route. I trust myself to read these sensations when I have them—the tiny vacuum flutters that are telling me *almost* and *maybe* and allowing me to hope that later, right before sleep, or while I'm stirring rice, the link will be achieved. Nothing. Though in the nothing I can't help hurriedly sorting names, thinking of people who might have given me this gift. Andra, Vicky, Sally . . . Why am I thinking of women? Am I so sure that no male I've known would think to get the thing, *any* thing, engraved? Whatever the reason, each person—there are others—asks me to think of a scene, an occasion. *Happy birthday! Congratulations! You did it!* But no—there's still nothing forthcoming. Which means that just like that I'm hedged in on all sides by my doubts and fears. Not just, *What kind of friend am I?* But also, worse, *If this, then what else?* How much of the rest of my living has moved out of reach? I can't help imagining an alternate scenario, a memory film of all that has fallen away, suffered erasure, or simply bit by bit waned. It would be almost everything, I realize. A whole forgotten existence rustling over the sprockets of the projector and flowering there on the screen. I imagine myself in all my banished incarnations: shaking hands with my parents' friends, or my friends' parents; shifting my weight from foot to foot in the cafeteria line behind my fourth-grade classmates; stomping in my rubber boots past the bus driver; taking notes year after year in big and small lecture halls as my professors make their points; eating sheet cake at farewell parties for coworkers; laughing on my end of the telephone at something someone said . . . Someone—who was it? What did the person say? Why did I laugh? I never had pants like that, glasses that spooned so hugely over my eyes; I never threw my arm around that fat boy and snickered into his ear. What room is that, what house, what little dog am I wrestling with on that carpet? Whose house, whose dog? World without end, amen. I have never said the word "coruscate" out loud in my life, I will swear on a Bible. I never put those rabbit ears over that girl in that crowd, and who is she, and who are all the others? I never skiied with wooden poles. Did I? It goes on, this merest moment's shudder of imagining. And then I'm there, here, still holding the thing, and Liam is looking on with interest. "What is it, Dad?" I smile and hand it over for him to look at. "A lighter," I tell him. "With my initials engraved on it." He looks impressed. "Wow—who gave it to you?" I look away, narrowing my eyes the way I do when I'm thinking hard. "I'm really not sure."

Photo: Father-in-Law

We have framed photographs of parents and grandparents from both sides of the family in various parts of the house—on the downstairs bookshelves, over Lynn's desk, and along the dresser top in the nondescript room that is really more like a wide passage to our bedroom than anything else. They are all so familiar that I rarely look at any one of them closely, though when I do it can be like a porthole suddenly opening onto some very deep business. But you are only given so many full-strength visitations in any one period—when you look, really look, and feel the stir of someone's likeness in its place and time. It's like breaking into a different zone—you actually grasp what that person was like when you were with them. Of course it never happens the same way twice. If the photo doesn't change, we do. Take the small framed color shot of my parents standing together that we keep on the bookshelf downstairs. This would have been taken ten or fifteen years ago, and for the longest time I thought of it as a recent picture. But then suddenly—I don't know what happened—it stopped being recent. At some moment when the room was empty or I was not paying attention, the two of them took a full step forward and then got into their same pose. Everything looked just the way it had, except that now the photo felt archival, loaded with change. And when I pass by it these days and have it in me to stop, I always remark on how young they look. A few years back they were my familiar parents, safely older, but now it's like I can reach right over. They are closing in on me.

One of the photos on the dresser outside our room, the one closest to the door, and therefore right in my line of sight day after day, is of my father-in-law, Earl Focht, as a young man. I knew Earl for several years before he died; he was in his seventies then. Looking out from the frame, like a dapper salesman come to the door on the first call of the day, is a young man. He is twenty or so, wearing a suit and tie with a pocket handkerchief. His hair is nicely combed, as hair always was. Handsome. Earl was often called, with joking familiarity, "Earl the Pearl" by members of Lynn's family. The tag catches something of the pretty-boy quality in the photo, and also the sense that he was a favorite, eager to please, much liked by the many women in the extended family and beyond. His mother-in-law, "Mag," adored him, to the point where she pestered Earl and Delores, her daughter, to take her along on their outings. It also remains much contested by his six daughters which of them was his favorite. And those were not the only women—one other in particular nearly broke up his marriage—but the young man in the frame knows none of that, which is of course part of the reason these old innocent images can sometimes overwhelm us.

Lately, though, I'm catching another kind of haunt. Every time I glance at Earl's face I can't not see the face of Matt Focht, the grown son of Lynn's brother Gary. I've seen Matt maybe five times in my life, and only twice, really, since he has grown up. But he is there, as sure as if he had cut off his long hair, shaved, and suited up. Resemblance, yes—why make a thing of it? But it nags at me. For I knew this photo of Earl for some time before Matt leapt into it, and now that he *is* there I can no longer not see him. I can't get Earl by himself anymore. And something very similar has happened with the framed portrait of my grandparents, Mike and Emilia, that we keep downstairs. It's a classic portrait: the two of them seem to me to be looking out not just from the familiar past but from a whole other era. They are like people unpacked from a battered old steamer trunk before the world found color. They stand, so young, but in that way the young once had of seeming old. Formal, unsmiling, prob-ably the same age as young Earl, but *historical.* That used to be the main thing that struck me when I bent to study their faces. But now, as with the other photo, all I see is resemblance. My grandmother's young face has been taken over by that of my niece Olivia—she is absolutely there, and by more than just virtue of facial similarity. Her presence itself feels like a feature of the resemblance—not that there is any known similar-ity between her personality and what we remember of Um. It's all so un-settling. As are the flashes—at this point they are still just that—that I get when I look at that picture of my parents standing together. There was a time when I could look at my father's face and see signs of his father—momentarily intense traces, as if someone had turned up the volume on resemblance—and that does still happen. But more commonly—I'd say a bit too often—I am seeing myself. Little glimpses in the photo, and more sustained visitations in the mirror. Not during the day, at which point I am habituated to myself, but in that first morning face-off, when I step into the downstairs bathroom with its big, well-lit mirror and flip the wall switch. He meets me and takes me in for a second or two before withdrawing. That face, and also the person behind the face. So familiar and strange at the same time. He vanishes, but I know he'll come again, and stay longer as time goes on. The photo on the living room shelf is safe by comparison, though it's true I've learned to avoid ambush by moving my gaze selectively when I pass through that room.

Stone Shard

It looks like a rough draft of an Indian arrowhead, a tapering piece of granite, flecked with gray and black and bits of what must be shiny quartz. Not much of anything, in other words, except for the associations. But what associations! The thing was presented to me years ago by a poet friend who had just returned from Ireland, where he and another poet, a great Irish poet, had gone together to the Martello tower in Dublin, and there, having etherized the custodian—how else could they have managed it?—had chipped off this gift for me. The tower is of course the place made famous by James Joyce, who used it for the opening scene of *Ulysses*. Young Stephen Dedalus is living there with his boorish friend Buck Mulligan, and the very first scene has Stephen and Mulligan up on the parapet in the "mild morning air," beginning what will be the most intimately documented day in literature. It's all so familiar, Mulligan shaving and blaspheming, both of them moving from place to place as they talk. I have made my way through the novel twice now, but I've read the opening sections many times more, so everything about the tower, with its sweeping view out over the bay and its great stone gun rests, feels deeply known. And the thought of my two friends in that place, performing that benign vandalism, has completely invaded this chunk of stone. This meditation piece. How easily the thoughts will start up and follow their tracks: to Joyce, his own connection to the place—like Dedalus, he too lived there briefly—and to all of Dublin, and then the transformation. For he wrote *Ulysses* mostly in Paris, re-creating the other city entire in his mind, vast miles of it, and bringing his tower up out of memory, and now, here, the gaze clarifies back to the stone on the desk. But it's all become more complicated still, more metaphysical maybe, since I saw the place myself later, a few years back. A group of us went to Dublin, and as a group we went to the tower, in the company of the Irish poet, who must do nothing but squire eager visitors like us to this sacred site. A great occasion, I thought, unable to resist prescripting. We parked near the water and stood to behold the looming shape on the hill. What a shock, what a collision it was, to wind up those circular stairs, the same ones Stephen ascends on the first page of the novel, and then to step onto the grand battlement with its massy stones and embedded iron rings, the view laid out on all sides in the clear air—and to find none of it quite equal to itself. The whole vast world for an instant seemed shrunken, less substantial in its grain and gravity—merely real. I'd had the same feeling before visiting historical sites with my family. The warping power of the long-imagined place. Maybe the others felt it too; I never asked. The visit seemed so important. Didn't we all suck in the sea air and gaze out over the flat pewter expanse? We posed ourselves this way and that and took photos. Then we looked out again, pointed and questioned. There was the headland, and the rock from which Mulligan dove. Where would he have laid his razor and mirror? For Joyce would have been exact. About all of it. Exact in the mind's remaking. But we had also passed the gift shop downstairs and so it was impossible not to think of the thousands and thousands who had trudged this same perimeter with their quotations and literary connections. How hard it is to get all the inner settings right, to take the world in straight. Joyce did not draw from life—he went into his memory, his language, and raised it up fresh: *looking towards the blunt cape of Bray Head that lay on the water like the snout of a sleeping whale.* He invented it. And I had invented it from his invention. And now here it was in itself, all of it, the vista out and below, the granite from the earth. A piece of which is on my desk, glittering under the desk lamp. It's impossible to see it now for what it is, and maybe I never could. Unless maybe at the moment when my friend first put it in my hand and I stared at it, saying, "What's this?" But probably not even then. For already there would have been some idea of intention—this was not just a stone, but a stone being given. As the poet Giuseppe Ungaretti wrote, "Between one flower plucked and the other flower given / the inexpressible nothing." Can anything stay? I have the photo album from our trip open here next to the shard. I remember how when our pictures first came back from being developed I was disappointed. We were only a few days returned and all the scenes were what we knew, but less. At that point they were mostly reminders. But now they have become things themselves. How did it happen? I turn the pages.

The images are so poignant, everything about them, the watery light, the expressions on our faces. I'm not simply looking at the photos, I'm also looking *through* something, like distance, like time—it's a clear layer. Then and now. I can almost pinch the difference between my thumb and forefinger. The changes in all of us—already. But the shard is something else. It's not personal. Staring at it I try to picture the man at his desk, in Paris—or Trieste, or Zurich, his other cities—turned so deeply in on himself. I imagine the arduous work—sometimes, it's said, no more than a sentence a day—what that was like, the stalled pen, the slow-moving point of pure attention: *Across the threadbare cuffedge he saw the sea hailed as a great sweet mother by the wellfed voice beside him.*

Brown Loafers

Some years ago, before the big operations for heart and cancer that under-mined him, long before he took his life, my great sad friend discovered the obsessive pleasures of fine clothing. Shirts, jackets, ties, accessories, shoes . . . They were his midlife capering, his solace, his way of contend-ing with what all of us at this stage contend with—the profound gut feel-ing of the ebb. He didn't restrict himself completely to fashion. There was a sporty car, too—he drove it top-down like a pasha, not at all concerned that doing this fulfilled so exactly the cartoon cliché of the male animal's last stand. He could joke about that. But the car was not field enough for his energies. He needed something he could fuss over. With clothes came the catalogs, the websites, the details and specs, not to mention the shop-ping safaris through the best shops in Manhattan. I fear I did not take him seriously enough. You see, I knew him from the time of jeans and loose shirttails, and could only suppose he was inviting us to watch him play a game. But if it was a game, he played it for keeps. When I visited him in his apartment in New York, as I did weekly for half a year when I came into the city to teach, he always led me to the closet in his study. I knew to give him this joy. I would sit on his couch while he lifted one shirt after another from its closet hanger and made me admire the stitch-ing on the collar, the hidden buttons; or a new jacket—"feel that lining, Sven"—or, especially, the shoes. My God, he was like a woman about his brogans, his spectators, his wingtips. But still I thought he was kidding, that we were just playing at serious and that he would soon shoot me the con-firming wink. As in, *You don't think that I—a serious writer and thinker—really care about this stuff?* But where was the wink?

If I misperceived my friend, he may have misperceived me as well. He thought I was much more interested than I was. I pretended to listen, pre-tended to care, and he believed me. My big mistake early on was mention-ing Lobb's—the elite English shoemaker. I knew the name only because a character in a Saul Bellow novel reportedly stopped off at Lobb's every time he was in England. I dropped the reference casually. And my friend was hooked. *I* knew about Lobb's? Well, that was fantastic. He could talk shoes with me, he could bring out his prizes, lecture me on soles and heel-work. And where there is such faith, such enthusiasm, one does not hurry to puncture it.

Then he took sick, entered his long season of operations and bodily humiliations. One of these—relatively minor—was that his feet became permanently swollen, which meant that some of his shoes no longer fit. This was how I came to own a beautiful pair of brown loafers. His presenting them to me was a sober ceremony. There was a long pause for gravitas, and a required period of beholding. We stood with the shoes on a chair between us. Finally he said—the first of many times—"Speaking of loafers, how's your father?" He was a humorist of rare nuance. Then he made me put them on. Cinderella. They seemed to fit perfectly, and about this he was as pleased as could be.

I should clarify now that these were not shoes from Lobb's. They were Italian. And what most impressed me was that each had, inset in the sole just ahead of the heel, a small brass plate reading JOHNSTON & MURPHY MADE IN ITALY. Truly nice-looking shoes. And they looked good on me—even my children said so. I fully expected to wear them and care for them and make them last forever. Alas, something was not quite right about the fit. When I walked, or even stood, they felt hard to me. If I wore them for a few hours my feet hurt, I found myself making strange compensatory maneuvers when I moved down the street. But I persisted. I would murmur that it was better to look good than feel good whenever Lynn shot me one of her narrowed looks. But after a few weeks I had to concede the truth: it was actually better to feel good than to look good. The loafers went into the closet. For a time my son, Liam, namesake of my friend, wore them. He was twelve then and they fit him perfectly. A year later his feet had grown too big. The loafers went back into the closet. I would slip them on if I was in a hurry, driving somewhere to do a quick errand.

When the news came that my friend, my boss, had killed himself, everything in my world shifted. Sadness itself is warm. After the sadness passed everything seemed colder, more matter of fact. I could still laugh, but it was harder to let go, I could feel the difference. Day after day I thought of things the man had said and done, many of them preposterous, some of them heartbreaking. Like making me stroke the collars of his shirts and the fancy linings of his new jackets. I would address him as if he were in the room. "You idiot—" And, "Speaking of loafers . . ." I did wear the shoes at his memorial service, and again my feet hurt. After that they stayed in the closet, but never out of sight. They still rest on a white wire rack and I see them every time I pass through the mudroom. Just the other day, more than a year after the service, I set them down and stepped into them. Testing, I suppose, wondering if they would feel different. Did I think that the shoes might have changed, or that I had? They were as hard as ever. Harder.

Walking with My Friend

Walking with my friend of twenty years I get sucked up into the moment, like I always do. We start in here or there with some bit of news, which takes us to the background story, or a joke, a poke in the ribs, an association, then more news. "Have you talked to Tom?" he asks, and I have or I haven't, and so we play the deck, laying the cards out as they come up, no order to speak of, except that we both know we'll somehow get to everything, and we almost always do. We've been going like this for years now, Sunday mornings, for a long time also walking his dog, but gradually she got old and unsteady, leaving us waiting somewhere on the path for minutes on end until she shuffled out, no comment from us on her absence, and then last fall she died. After that we couldn't take the same walk anymore, the sadness was too much for my friend; we found other places. But the basic rhythms continue, so familiar, and we have enough to talk about that I hardly ever step to the side, though I do notice every so often how the themes change—more about our parents getting older, and more time given to complaining about the yoke of teaching, the papers, the classes, the students. But for all of that I hardly ever go flashing backward. We might remember something, a person or an event, but I don't usually need to bring back the whole picture, the feeling of the time. Enough just to brush across the surface as we do. We both move on top of the many layers of knowing each other, though they are all there in the conversation somehow, in the tone of the references, the speed of the asides, in the assumptions that fill our pacing with densities that no one eavesdropping could possibly get. Untouched, but there, are the nights and nights when we drank and ate and pumped ourselves up with ambition and argument, as are all the rifts and misfires, the jealousies. The parade of rooms and apartments and new friends brought in, manuscripts given back, endless bluster and insult, and insult masked as bluster, so sharp sometimes that Lynn would ask later how we could stand it. "He was being serious." "You hurt his feelings." This would make me step outside the tangle of private assumptions and replay the scene. At which point it always seemed true, I had inflicted hurt. Phone calls and e-mails followed, patches and balm and self-justification. But walking along the side of the road, Mystic Lake a few hundred yards off, a cold glitter of light on the water, we don't think of any of it, or not in those terms. Nothing but the news, the jumps and connections—until suddenly, with no warning, nothing but the fast scraping sound of shoes on ice, my friend goes from being by my side to gaping up at me from a sprawl in the snow. I hurry over to give him my hand, but he won't take it. He is laughing, but I see him testing for hurt as he uncrumples and makes his way to his feet. I note the shine under the hair, which has gone gray and thinned, but which still looks debonair when he combs it back from his forehead. We hardly pause before moving on, as if to pause would be to give the thing an edge, a point of purchase.

Photo, Ring

The photograph was taken by my niece, Liam's cousin Olivia, during a trip they took to Latvia with their grandparents late this past summer—it was the first time either of the younger kids had been to the Old Country. The image grabbed me as few images do, and I took it from the small stack she presented us with and right away pinned it to the kitchen bulletin board. For starters, it's a very "cool" shot. I told Liam he should hurry up and cut an album so that he can use it as the cover. It has that kind of feel—very *jazz*. In the immediate foreground, taking up half the photo, is Liam from the back. Just head and shoulders. He is tilted forward, a jacket slung over his left shoulder, wearing his black hat with his long red ponytail bunching out underneath. The vista in front of him, slightly tilted, is of Riga, part of the Old City. We see a cobbled street narrowing toward a bright white church of Mittel-European vintage. On the left, two building facades in the classic nineteenth-century European style, one salmon colored, the other a rich light green. Two new-looking cars are parked in front of the buildings. For me the image is completely saturated. Of course, this is the landscape, the setting, that both my parents, and their parents, grew up in. The air is clear, but the atmosphere is pure narration—full of the vibration of all the stories I heard growing up. But also, this is a street I know I've walked, probably many times. For the Old City is not large, and I have been there on three separate occasions (years ago) to visit my grandmother, my father's mother, while she was still alive. The photo gives me a strong visceral sense of the future meeting the age-old layered, and I can hardly sort through the implications.

This trip with the grandparents, though just a week long, was a success. Liam came back flush with his new experience, his stories, his pictures, his gifts for friends. We broke off chunks of Latvian chocolate and sampled from his bag of *gotiņas,* or "little goats," a granular caramel sweet wrapped like a present in thick colored paper. But the first thing I noticed, long before he showed us his various souvenirs, right after hugging him at the airport, was that he was wearing a braided silver Latvian ring. My parents had bought it for him at a special shop (I remembered going to the same place so many years before), and he flashed it around proudly. "I had a ring like that," I said. "Remember?" He thought maybe he did. I felt a distinct pang when I saw it. I'd had two of these beautiful rings in my life and had lost both of them. The first time there was some explanation, though I've forgotten it. But the more recent loss was a complete mystery to me. One moment I had it, the next it was gone. This was maybe a year ago. The ring *had* always been slightly loose. I wondered if it had not slipped off when I was swimming at Walden. I kept feeling around in my pockets for it for a long time after. Well, we lose things and we don't always know how. But there are categories of things, and rings are different from wallets or keys. They are adornments, but they are also pure symbol, and the loss of a symbol is not nothing. I suppose I should now be able to say what my braided ring symbolized to me. I can't. It was not just Old Country, or family, though both are part of it. Symbols always exceed the sum of their parts.

What I'm writing here is not a story, and not quite a parable, though it could be either if what follows can be seen to mean something. But I don't know that I can quite work it into shape.

Less than a week after Liam's return I was going through the mudroom closet, moving old shoes and boots to store the air conditioner for the winter. I happened to tip one boot on its side, and when I did I heard a hard little *pock* against the hardwood—it was my Latvian ring. I went still for a moment. Then I picked it up and slipped it right onto the waiting finger, as if it had just come off right then and there. It was the sweetest satisfaction—that of restoration. And the rest of the day, and maybe the next, I would catch myself extending my left hand like a recently affianced sorority girl just to look. Only I was not looking so much to admire as to attest—and reattest—that it was really there. That simple gesture made it clear to me how much it meant—not just the finding, but also the timing of the find. I had the distinct sense of something closing up right, as when a loosely sewn thread is pulled tight to finish a stitch. My parents, their old deep world, my son, and the tangle of my feelings for all of it. When I study Olivia's photograph, I can feel Liam's forward movement, the velocity of the arrow; when I touch my thumb to the braid and give the ring a turn, I know the exact circumference of the target.

Rufus and Lenny

"Hope is the thing with feathers," wrote Miss Dickinson. But so, I hate to say, is hopelessness. And these are the hopelessness twins, Rufus and Lenny, our two cockatiels, acquired one soon after the other—Rufus first—in fits of childish avidness. "I'll take care of it, I'll do everything!" is a promise that surely ranks with "Don't worry, I'll take it out—" on the spectrum of unlikely bets. Rufus and Lenny, those bedraggled agitators, are parked right now in adjacent cages at the foot of the attic stairs, right by the street-side window, so that their mindless squawks and tin-cutting cheeps are the first thing anyone hears rounding the corner onto our street. They're certainly the first thing I hear in the morning, even if the bedroom door is closed—unless it's the viscera-torquing plaint of Scruffy, our cat, who pads right to my side of the bed before announcing himself. Writing this now, listening to the noises at the bottom of the attic stairs, I realize that I'm almost never *not* hearing these birds when I'm at home, which is most of the time. If it's not the vocal irritations, then it's the thudding aerodynamic bursts as they try, one or the other (never both at once) to do what birds ought to be doing, except within an enclosure not much bigger than a large toaster oven. The hurling and banging are wrenchingly metaphorical, and I wish they would stop, wish I could let them out the window and away; I wish—well, I confess I sometimes hear the voice of our friend Terry Bowman in my ear, Terry, who said, "Hey, just twist their heads off and flush 'em."

But there's more to that story. You see, Terry is the father of Liam's great friend Lewis and used to be married to Lenora, a thin, nervous, chain-smoking—strange—woman who would show up at the boys' soccer games with several of her many birds on her shoulders, or swerving around on their little leashes, wearing their "flight suits" (diapers). So when Terry gives us his wry recommendations, they are not without backstory. In any case, it was Lenora who first got my boy hooked on the idea of cockatiels, and he cajoled and cajoled and . . .

Rufus, bird number one, was given that name because Liam had played someone named Sir Rufus in his school play. His first weeks as our new family pet were a kind of honeymoon. Liam was so delighted, so proudly proprieterial, that we looked past the pasty splats that started showing up on surfaces everywhere in the house. Well, we didn't *look past* so much as we excused, all of us taking turns with the newly repurposed baby wipes. Nor did I get as upset as I might have when I discovered that Rufus had one afternoon eaten the dust jacket spines off a good many of the books in my lit-crit shelves. We bore with it all because of Liam, and because the bird was cute. Back in the days when he still had his pilot's license, he would land anywhere and everywhere with fierce immediacy, the velocity of his arrival countered by the sudden regal stillness of his perching demeanor. He liked armrests, shoulders, heads, anything that was rounded and protruding; only when he landed on a shelf or a table was there a sense that he was scrabbling, uneasy, about to fly off again—which is usually what happened unless he landed near my books. On a shoulder, though, he would turn his head sideways a full forty-five degrees—these birds don't seem able to turn their heads just a little—and then raise or lower his beautiful little crest, his pompadour, and with unnerving precision flash his little beak down on some microscopic bit of lint. It was winning. For a week or two. Then less so. And finally not at all. These were not the limitations of the bird that we discovered, but our own. "Look at Roofie!" became "Will somebody get that fucking bird out of here?" very quickly. And thus he was put in stir, where he remained, his only activity besides squawking (and something else, which I'll get to) being the sorting and flinging of seeds. They carpet the upstairs corridor no matter how often we vacuum, crunching under our shoes, sticking in our socks, both of which I could tolerate if I didn't have to hear them drop. *Tick, tick, tick.* This sounds astonishingly petty, but it's true and I have to say it. No matter where in the house I am—reading, trying for a nap, whatever—I hear the impact of those little casings on the hardwood floor. It's like that Edgar Allan Poe story "The Tell-Tale Heart." *Tick, tick, tick.*

And now, with Lenny, the tick rate is doubled. What were we thinking? I can tell you. It was the second-child rationale. *Maybe if Rufus has a companion* . . . Well, we made a mistake. Several. We thought that since Liam had a bird, and since our daughter, Mara, professed to love it, we could give her a cockatiel for *her* birthday. I remember how pleased we were, Liam and I, to drive to the PETCO in Burlington on our mission. And also how deflated we were when the man told us that most of the cockatiels were gone, he had only a few left. We looked. None of the birds in the cage had the vigor or self-satisfied bearing of our Rufus, that was obvious. We adjusted our expectations down, and down again, until they came to fit a white bird in the corner of the cage. He, or she—we didn't know, the man didn't know, we still don't know—had what looked like a medieval monk's tonsure in back of the crest. A bald spot. "What's that?" I asked. "Oh, that's where one of the other birds picked at him. They do that. It'll grow back." Two years later, Lenny (named after Leonard Cohen by Mara) still sports his spot. Which is not his (or her) only liability. Unlike Rufus, Lenny never "got with the program." He was certainly no Rufus. Never one for flight or socializing with humans, the poor thing spends most of his time just sitting on his perch, staring—at least when any of us are around to observe. I have tried to sneak up a few times, to see if there might be other activity when humans are out of sight. Mostly not. It does seem, though, that Rufus has in some way adopted Lenny. If I lean in toward Lenny's cage, for instance, Rufus will hop in my direction and expel a nasty little hiss. Go away! But, best for last, there is that other, aforementioned business. At odd hours, often in the afternoon, the grating cheeps will taper away, and there will be an interlude of . . . something. I remember the first time I heard it—I was reading. There came the gentlest burbling sound, as soothing as the other sounds were grating, and it went on and on, unchained melody, water purling over stones, wind in the leaves. Tiptoeing over, I could see that the birds were side by side in their cages, but I couldn't tell exactly what they were doing. It was some kind of intimate fussing—but apart, as in parallel play. Curious as I was, I did not interrupt. I stood to the side and just listened. It was Mara who later set me straight. "You know what's going on," she said—Mara is very straight about these things—"I don't know how they do it, but someone told me that when they make those noises they're masturbating." *Masturbating!* What could that possibly be like for a bird? I was more than a little shocked. But later, thinking about it, I started to feel glad. Good for them! We all have interludes of joy in our lives—Rufus and Lenny should get something, too. What they were doing was another kind of flying. It was samizdat. I felt that much less guilty about the cages. I also felt—this will sound strange—somehow closer to both of them.

In Another City

I'm in another city, staying at another of those inns that medium-sized college towns seem to specialize in, the old house on the corner with the turrets and the big porch and the dead silent entryway, the antiques—the decor always represents someone's collecting passion—the little bowls of potpourri set out on every surface, always making me think of my old history of art class, Professor Spink's lecture on Westerners' "fear of the void." In those gloomy, tasteful rooms I unfailingly get anxious and depressed, in spite of the ridiculous strategies I come up with in my bid to just this once outwit the inevitable. I set out my projects, papers to read, notebook, pens, whatever . . . But no, something about being away from my haunts, at the mercy of my hosts, scheduled to talk or read, and therefore scheduled to be polite to dozens of people, certain to face an underpopulated room where half the people present have in one way or another been strong-armed to be there (the students made to sign attendance sheets to get credit, the nervous-looking kin of whoever is hosting, the skeptical department members . . .), having to get through the intolerable "stand-around" after when obligatory-feeling compliments and brain-twister questions are offered up, during which time the host is quietly double-checking that the special invited ones know what time to get to the restaurant . . . Thank God for alcohol, I say, though saying that reminds me of being in Indiana last month, at a small Christian college, where one of the department members hosted dinner after the reading and offered the choice of iced tea or cranberry juice. "Or we have water."

This most recent trip, yesterday and the day before, was smoother than most, but even with the best hosts and the easiest venue there was no escaping. I found the void, the void found me. I opened my eyes in the predawn and there it was. A clenching in the gut, the kind that makes it unthinkable to stay confined in the room, never mind that it's many hours before anything starts. I have to get out for a walk, and I do. Right away.

In fact, I'm surprised by *how* "right away." I step out of my room and in a minute I'm on the street. Nothing intervening. Room, street. And of course there's not a soul to be seen. Just the damp air and the blue-bagged morning paper on the walkway. The sensation is always the same: I'm in a science fiction movie called *Last Man Left on Earth*. All humans except me have been anesthetized and taken away. Just these hedges and sidewalks, those blinking red traffic lights up ahead, block after block, the color haloed by the light mist. Inevitably, I head toward town, still half in the sole-survivor fantasy, until at last some car guns its engine streets away and I'm merely myself in a faraway city, hearing my steady walking sounds and, every few moments, the timer clicks from the lights at the intersections. And then at some point I always think that all these different morning streets are a single morning street, and all this solitude is one solitude, my other life, which feels more persuasive and more real to me at these moments than the one I'm ostensibly living, with children whose faces I can't quite remember, a wife who moves like a mist behind her doings, and really, what could be more real, more etched in, than the droplets on that hedge—I never see droplets that clearly at home—or the notice taped to the window of the local realty office advertising the Red Cross blood drive? It goes on like this, on and on, and walk as I might I can never step free of the gloom—going back to my room doesn't help, reading doesn't help. A shower, some coffee? No, it takes the day being over; it takes leaving the city behind, and with it all my clamor about how much I enjoyed my visit—it takes saying good-bye to my hosts at the airport, and watching them in their cars as they circle back around to the exit.

The Finger Writes

The smallest detail in the heart of the day. I was driving in the sleety rain earlier, coming up Massachusetts Avenue, stuck in stop-start traffic, in an unsettled mood, exhausted from a very early waking, but agitated in my mind. I had just come from a lunchtime session at Harvard during which the critic James Wood worked his way through a single passage of Saul Bellow's story "Zetlin," proceeding, it seemed, almost phrase by phrase, which was fatiguing in one way, but also gratifying, forcing the attention onto the slightest shifts of emphasis. It left me adjusted to a similar wrench size. And it also—by example, because it was Wood—made me feel that I should go home and work: there can be no letup. The inner struggle was on—give it up, or force it? Or give it up for a little while and *then* force it? I had no answer forthcoming, just my growing irritation at a pair of yellow school buses that had the left lane locked up. It seemed like every time I saw an opening ahead, a break, one or the other would drop back or pull up just enough to box me out. We went on this way for long minutes and the rain was just flinging off the wipers with water splashing up on all sides. The windows, of course, fogged. I felt completely trapped and frustrated, with all my best energy going into strategizing how to cut past those buses. No dice. Another light, the long one at Porter Square. I may have talked to myself; I may have said "this too shall pass," or something inane. I forget. What I remember is that right in the dead thick of it all, when my mood was at its most combustible, I happened to lean forward and look up. Though the windows of the bus were completely misted over, I could make out indistinct moving shapes—like seeing the slow shuffle of carp at the bottom of a pool. And then, just before the light turned, just before I once again hustled to get a jump, I saw a finger, a finger so small I couldn't picture what kind of child it might belong to, draw a crooked circle in the window just above me. So slow and careful. And such a sweet shape. Followed—slowly, slowly—by a dot in the middle and two opposing sets of whiskers. One little triangle for an ear, then the other. And then we were off. Except that this time I was marveling. All the way up Mass Ave I did not shake those buses for at least another mile—we were in tandem all the way to the Arlington line. But now, with every stop and start, I glanced up and saw it there, already losing that first clean startling look, but still intact. Here was a whole caravan of traffic, the jumble of a rainy day, but now it had a focus. And somehow, who knows why, when I saw that finger it was like someone reached inside and tapped the dial, put me square on my station.

Archive

You can't see it, but I'm shaking my head and smiling as I write this. My archive. My "archive" is a do-it-yourself shelving unit on the other side of a plastered-in chimney column in the attic, stocked with about twelve of those cutaway magazine holders, each about three inches wide at the base. These are roughly sequenced on the top two shelves and stuffed with old magazines and folded newspapers. They could be said to represent the best part of about twenty-five years of literary endeavor. Under these I've arranged three shelves' worth of spine-out quarterlies and single issues of the magazine I edit. On top and piled in no order whatsoever are bundles of manuscript—copyedited versions of texts deemed somehow too important to just throw away. Beside them is a clear plastic bin stuffed with letters and documents relating to literary pursuits—responses from editors to queries, notes from readers and fellow writers about this or that publication or event. That's pretty much it. You wouldn't know it, but it's a vast improvement on the system that was in place until about two years ago, which was a willy-nilly array of large cardboard boxes containing the same materials jammed together in no order whatsoever. One day I couldn't stand the chaos anymore. There followed a long obsessive weekend of sorting and stacking to mark the transition from boxes to shelf organization. I sat on the floor unfolding old sections of the *Boston Globe* and paging through journals that had gone under years before; I skimmed my own prose, a paragraph here, a paragraph there, grimacing but also making that "what do you know?" expression that is the highest accolade of self to self. I also peeked at old correspondence and—surprise—marveled at the transience of human affairs. Our lives, *my* life! Then, finally, at the end of the weekend, I uncracked my knees one last time and stepped back to take in what I had accomplished. And . . . we need a word, there must be a word—something with the imported thrust and nuance of *schadenfreude* or *cafard*—that signifies the failure of some great initiative to deliver any of its intended satisfaction. "Fizzle," I'd say, or "flop"—but both words sound silly and small. I'll think of something. The point is that after all that work, after two days of purposeful high-speed self-tourism, I stood in the center of my attic feeling completely, utterly deflated. This was all meant to have the opposite effect. I was hoping for a private celebration, a confirmation of labors and hard-won, if small, attainments. I did the psychological math. Every last one of those folded newspaper tearsheets or individual magazines or journals represented something. Each was the vindication of hours at the desk, and these of course followed many more hours of reading and note taking—the coffee! the concentration!—and then there were the hundreds of anxious deadline exchanges with copy-editors, the phone calls, the faxes, my excusing myself from dinner again and again because I *had* to take this call from Pat, get back to Ann. These publications were—every last one—things I had been shamefully keen for. How many times did I wake myself early to get the paper, or loiter behind the curtain while the mailman came up the street, or in some cases even drive to Out of Town News in Harvard Square? Vanity, pride (in the biblical sense), ego, narcissism—no shortage of words for *this!*

My private archive logic was simple. If each of these separate publications represented its own proud occasion, what could be more exalting than their ordered assembly? Here: the harvest of my own finest fruits, a distillation, an . . . archive! I labored in the warmth of my anticipation. I finally understood why people bought champagne. But—and this is the place for the extended drumroll—when the *ta-da* moment at last arrived, when I moved back and took one of those significant life-punctuating breaths, looking down and then looking slowly up again—I found myself staring right into what could have been the back end of a junkman's truck. I confronted bunches of old yellowed newspapers squeezed into file boxes, drab spines of indistinct-looking journals, tattered envelopes in a see-through box. Paper! Suddenly all I could think of were those hundreds—yes, literally hundreds—of basements and attics and library culs-de-sac I had sifted through years ago when I was a book dealer. My partner, George, and I used to go out on calls day after day, week after week, to the homes of retiring professors, or the widows of retired professors, and to ragtag book sales, auctions, and liquidations. We bent and knelt and hunkered and inhaled book dust and nudged each other excitedly or skeptically as we carried stacks of someone's precious holdings into the light. There were books, of course, always books, but also magazines—and papers just like this. We inspected these products of private aspiration with the cold eye of the market, weighing them in the balance and . . . *mene mene tekel upharsin*. When were they not wanting? And now all of a sudden I was that self, an emissary, looking at this other self, his deeds, in the present, but also able to project far too easily into the indeterminate future when it would be my proxy delivering ultimate judgment. My archive. My life. Who wouldn't want a drink, or three? Saint Thomas Aquinas is said to have had a mystical experience in late life after which he observed: "All I have written seems like so much straw to me." Not that I compare myself to the venerable doctor of the church—he has whole colleges named after him—but the perspective is there to be considered. In the two years since its completion I don't know that I've visited the archive more than once or twice. I pretty much avoid that part of the attic.

Papa

Hemingway, Hemingway, Heming—and there it was. I was right! Which, alas, isn't true as often as it used to be. Time was when I could find my way in the heart of the night, room unlit, to the shelf and the place on the shelf where *any* one of my books might be. Book radar. I attributed it to my years working in bookstores—there is, how to put it, a *thing* that happens. I've never had to use any serious kind of ordering with my own books because I've never needed to—it has always been enough to know the basic shape, jacket hue, and associative proximity to other books. All worthy books have presence. So in my better days I would have instantly pictured the wide off-yellow spine pressed up (for no good reason) next to the unread paperback of Gottfried Keller's *Green Henry,* which my friend Tom Frick was always urging on me back in the seventies, and also because it's a novel that one of Peter Handke's characters reads obsessively. I will read it before I die. But never mind, the point is that although I've had a few misses in recent years, real head shakers, I nailed the book this time. I was able to hurry back down the stairs and hand it to Liam before he lost whatever impulse had led him to say, "Do you have any stuff by Hemingway?" We'll see how that goes.

But I bring up Hemingway for another reason. Hemingway allows me to ask, again—and I'm always asking—what makes the difference between mere coincidence and something slightly more? Unrelated events strike thematic sparks all the time. But there are also coincidences that surpass the "mere," that are overtly provocative. Yesterday was a day of provocations, and Hemingway had a part to play. Two hours after handing Liam that copy of the *Selected Stories,* the venerable old Scribner's hardcover—first taking a few minutes to read through the listing of contents and lightly pencil-mark the stories I thought he might like—I was in my office at Boston University, sifting through a small stack of mail, mostly submissions, that had come to the magazine I edit. My daughter, Mara, was with me, helping me read through a stack of poetry manuscripts. Suddenly I was sitting up in my chair. "Hey—" I scanned the letter in my hand more carefully. "Look at this!" I passed it to Mara so that she could join my surprise. It was a cover letter for a story submitted by someone identifying herself as the granddaughter of Ernest Hemingway. Vanessa Hemingway. She had impressive letterhead. And Mara was appropriately impressed. That was when I told her that I had just a short time before given her brother, Liam, a book of Hemingway's stories to look at. Mara has always loved coincidences. She would probably make more of this than I could. I almost wanted to caution her: *now don't start thinking life is all mystical or anything.* But after shaking her head a few times and saying "that's so strange," she went back to her reading. Five minutes later I interrupted her with a snort. Now it was me getting big ideas. I was holding in my hand a completely unrelated submission postmarked . . . Ketchum, Idaho. "Now *this* is weird," I said, waving the envelope. "This is from Ketchum, Idaho. That's where Hemingway shot himself." "Oh my God—" Mara was obviously intrigued. "That is *really* strange, Dad." But as I've said, there's no place to take these things, nothing to find. Three Hemingway scores in a two-hour period. If authors had stock for sale, I suppose I might have considered calling my broker. But they don't, and I don't have a broker, either. Instead, my daughter and I shared a long pause and considered the strangeness of life from our respective perspectives. End of story.

Except that it isn't. Three hours later I was in a suit standing in the John F. Kennedy Presidential Library and Museum on the harbor, getting ready to play my part in a literary event. I had arrived early, as instructed, and had met the person I was to "interview." Our library host took us both up to the seventh floor and showed us the Kennedy reception room, where members of the Kennedy family greet special guests at library functions. This was not one of those functions. Still, we toured the room and admired the spectacular view of the harbor below. I was inspecting a photograph said to be the late president's favorite picture of Jacqueline—she is astride a galloping horse, hair blowing—when the host said, "You might be more interested in the room downstairs where we keep the Hemingway collection." Did I register the slightest spectral motion just then? I can't be sure. Certainly I did a private double take. I said that yes, absolutely, I would be *very* interested. And so we were conducted in a keyed elevator down to another floor and led into a low-lit plush room with books and labeled archive files on two walls, a long glass case by the door, and a truly impressive lion's hide rug with a massive head and bared grimace, on top of which rested a big steamer trunk on the side of which was, crudely lettered, the name: H E M I N G W A Y. The host then called to our special attention various manuscript pages displayed under glass, including—this was clearly the one that interested him—a page from *A Farewell to Arms.* The three of us leaned over. It was the well-known section in which Hemingway has Lieutenant Henry reflecting that life eventually breaks everyone, but that those who survive find the mended places are even stronger than before. There was a scrawl on the bottom of the page from Hemingway's friend F. Scott Fitzgerald suggesting he end the novel with this passage, and another scrawl under that, in Hemingway's own hand—the host liked this very much—that read: "Kiss my ass!" As it happens, that was the end of the Hemingway theme. But I carried it with me the rest of the day. I found this to be an unusual degree of coincidence. I couldn't—and still can't—shake the thought that there was something intended for me in this. Two events are a lift of the eyebrow, three a pensive shake of the head; four just might indicate that an important phrase is being put into italics.

Reading Oneself

A former student asks if I will read her book manuscript and I agree. I want to honor the friendship, the faith, all that work we did together. She had been my student years ago, so many years that I can barely recall the rhythms of our correspondence or what kinds of things I was then commenting on, but I remember the feeling of the work clearly enough, and now she's brought it all around—finished, she hopes. We meet in a Starbucks in Cambridge. She greets me clutching a big black cardboard box in both hands, and my first reaction is a suppressed wince. Before I've really even looked at her I've taken in the thickness of the box, I'm already wondering if it's packed to the top. "Oh, it's not all the way up to the top," she laughs. Have I given myself away? "No, no," I say. Then, a chuckle, "Think of *Moby-Dick*." She sits down. We think of *Moby-Dick*. I give her an inspecting look, tap my fingers on the lid of the box between us on the table. We smile real smiles. All that work. "Hey," she says, taking off the lid. "I want you to see this." On top of the manuscript is an old college evaluation form—my final comments on our semester together. Typewritten. When M and I worked together I was still using a Selectric II. Seven or eight years, an era. She wants me to take out the page and read what I wrote. "This is what helped to keep me going," she says. I nod, but in truth I never believe anything I say can have that kind of effect on a person. But how wonderful if true. As I start to read, slowly, aware of her watching me, I'm also aware that I'm preemptively girded against something. The return of my own rhetoric? I work to connect with the slightly strange-looking typed sentences. And suddenly there's this feeling, I've had it before—more and more in recent years. I am reading something I've written and I not only don't recognize the sentences—they've gone from me—I also don't quite map to the mind that produced them. It's very much like catching your shopwindow reflection for a split second before you realize it's you. Almost always, the shock is negative. I look like *that?* With these sentences it's the opposite. My eyes catch sight of what my hand did. Reading, I actually admire the images, the figures of speech, the confidence of the rhythm. Not the rhythm I would write in now. But I feel it as distinct. And with that comes the dim—because still mainly suppressed—question: Was I better then? Was I sharper, more concise? I suppress, but not because I have an answer. I don't know, will never know. The fact is that we write as we are. You can doctor a thought, change or improve an image, but you can't really impersonate a style. Visiting an earlier prose version of yourself is like facing an old photograph; the looking is mainly about taking in the differences. But then we also change how we judge, don't we? Contemplating the photograph, I retaliate against my younger, sharper face by finding it naive, without character. Reading myself, I recognize an obviousness that I like to think I've been getting past. I do believe I'm better now, further along in hacking away the approximations, more confident of what a sentence can do. All that. It's the necessary logic of the inverse: as we lose our best youth, we get closer and closer to real expressiveness. It's sad, though, that we usually attack our best subjects before we know what to do with them, and attacking them wears them out for our later purposes. What to do now with all this style?

The German Poet

The German poet came to join us at our writing residency with his wagonload of vowels and his gestures all slightly skewed from ours. When he stood at the lectern to read his work that evening I felt the true presence of poetry in the room. It was in what was spoken, of course, and, even more, there in the spaces between lines and the shifts that happened with an image, or just after. But these effects did not account for the poetry so much as testify that it was poetry that was making its way into the language. The poetry was what I located *behind,* in back of, the words. The speech did not make the poetry, but the poetry, the claim of another consciousness, another state of mind, set the words into order. And I understood then, as I have understood before, and forgotten before, why it is that we need the poet. The poet speaks on behalf of the least tangible, but also possibly deepest, awareness that we possess. But it is an awareness so elusive, so fitful in its arrivals, that we mainly live in forgetfulness. Poetry is the one reminder, the line of connection. The poem is a memory flash of a meaning that exceeds us, that hovers almost completely out of our reach. If we could possess it—and we can't except in glimpses—we would know that being, consciousness, is not for nothing, even if it is clearly bracketed by the moments of our birth and death. Being contains the solution for itself, the explanation, and poetry happens at those moments when being connects with its principle. It need not be dictated by a Muse, but it does not, ever, arrive out of daylight consciousness. Poetry is an intrusion, an over-and-above that sets almost everything else for the moment at naught. I am not a poet, but I have felt the touch of poetry, enough that I understand it as a power, a matter for awe. The experience of a true poem is the experience of being awestruck. By the words, the beauty, but more by the revelation in the self of an awareness, a feeling, that temporarily banishes other considerations.

For a period, several years ago, I took a train from Boston to New York to teach an evening class. I always left midday, arriving in the late afternoon. I would begin the ride with my books and papers, getting ready. I read and took notes, and the local countryside slid by, then the long Connecticut seacoast. At that point I would always break from my work and look out at the water, the islands, the steadily elapsing contour line of the shore. I would stare and stare until I felt myself grow drowsy. Then, without fail, as if I were programmed to it, I would take off my glasses and close my eyes and slip quickly into what felt like the sweetest oblivion. I never measured how long I slept—the duration didn't matter. What mattered was that every time I opened my eyes and looked around, resonating with the vibration of the train, I would feel that I had awakened in a different place in myself, in a state that felt very strange compared to my usual state but that was at the same time more deeply familiar than anything. This happened to me week after week, and each time long minutes passed before it ebbed away, though the idea of minutes was something I came to later. While the sensation lasted I felt myself rested and alive and fully contained. Somehow my fellow passengers were a part of it; they were inside the same enclosure. We were in league, not just traveling together but *traveling together,* part of some momentum that could not be undone by anything. Of this I felt completely sure. The vibration in my body guaranteed it. It did not matter that that woman was going to meet her sister and that the man across from her had a conference, or that I would be teaching a class that night that would begin and end, would be a success or a failure. Those considerations were all outside the envelope, mattering but mattering not. The spindly trees flashing by, though, those were grown at the root into the secret—they mattered—as did the watery lit-up clouds composed right then in the moment, never to make those designs again, but somehow also lasting. As I was, as we all were. I felt this not once but many times, and each time I sat in my seat and let my gaze float from the window to the profiles of the people riding in the car. Each time I asked myself how I could keep this certainty, never forget it, this most useful knowledge that I could not explain. I would then assure myself that it was strong enough, that I would know how to call it to mind. But each time, by day's end, it had slipped away.

When the German poet read his poems I felt it come back. From one line to the next, from image to image, it rose up in me—so near, so ready. Safe! I felt the certainty touch me and I understood again what I had forgotten, that art is set into circulation like a gift, not to be owned or awarded or banished or taught. I looked down from my perch in the auditorium and studied the poet, who seemed momentarily enlarged by the authority of what he was reading, and I saw how he stepped back, almost subsided into himself when the applause was finished. But he still had the glow on him, the shimmer of whatever place he had just traveled through. After the reading, we bundled up and went to eat and drink, a small group of us. The poet had all but fully returned to us; he was ready for his cocktail, his cut of meat, and he was more than happy to tell his stories about writers he had known and places he had been. But the writers, the places, they were all back on this side, part of the world we had in common.

What Is the Poet?

What is the poet? Who is the poet? Those grand old philosophical posers. And to answer philosophically would take us right to the heart of things. But I don't know how much philosophy I have in me today. Really I threw out the questions so that I could write about going to see Adam Zagajewski at Boston University the other night. My experience started with a miss. Looking all around me, I walked right by the man himself as I went into the seminar room. He was standing there at the door, two feet away, but I was so fixated on my long-ago impression of his impossibly black and bristling eyebrows that I discounted any other resemblance. The man by the door—I thought this a moment later—was what Adam Zagajewski would look like if his eyebrows were white. I took a few more strides before working out that eyebrows, composed of hair, could change color. By then it was too late, I was in the room, seated. I'd gone right to the front.

I like to be able to see my readers, to study their little gestures and tics up close, as if they might help me answer some of my questions. Not that appearances give up the deepest secrets. But neither are they negligible. A poet's face—how could it not be the most interesting thing in the world? Eyes, mouth. Eyes and mouth together. The repertoire of expressions, and Zagajewski's seemed especially rich. In him—this was clear right away— the current of irony runs steady. Almost everything he said when he was not reading his poems, but introducing them, or, later, responding to questions from the audience, needed to be read against that horizon, its meaning altered. Not necessarily inverted—irony is not so simple—but revealed as complex, shaded. So many gradations of expression are possible here, and I'm sure the Poles are expert. So much so, in fact, that I wonder that they don't go half mad among us literalist Americans. Maybe this is why members of various cultures and ethnicities cluster together— not so much out of fear or chauvinism, but to be able to speak in their full register, in their real voices.

I'm making it sound as if Zagajewski is all dark humor and understatement, but above it and below it, on either side, and maybe seeping through it, too, is everything else. The lyrical. Love, loss, and memory. The world addressed, detail by detail. This is stronger than the irony. You only have to look at the man's face, his mouth, which is not an ironist's whetted blade, but a sad, exposed feature, upper lip pushed forward so that at times it seems to be pouting, or getting ready to whistle. I studied that face as I listened, and along with the face the hands, the fingers, which seemed uneasy in the world, not at all jaded from work and the handling of things.

This poet so clearly lives inside. He has the look of a man who is always listening, even as he talks to you—as if he's also trying to hear a conversation in the other room. He gave a beautiful reading. I was very glad I had come. For the poems, of course, but I can get to the poems better by myself. No, I was glad to be near that power, its very special consistency. As he read, I thought, by no means for the first time, that real poets are very few. They are, Baudelaire was right, like those big seabirds—pelicans— that from time to time land on decks of ships, where sailors make great sport with them, sticking pipes in their beaks . . . But let's not forget the same birds once their wings have lifted them, when the ships are again miniatures. I pictured this one, climbing the air slowly, churning, finally pushing his head with its great white eyebrows up through a thick, woolly cloud cover, looking slowly from side to side as he continued on.

As Above: Saul Bellow

When I left for Italy with my family on the Fourth of July in 2005, I had only one contemplative agenda—to pull together my thoughts on Saul Bellow, whose death back in April had been such a milestone event in the larger literary world, but had also left our immediate community, here in Boston, with such a palpable sense of void. I didn't want to write the usual hagiography. I'd read a good dozen of these in recent months. What was there to add? Before I even got on the plane, then, I found myself brewing something different. A road journal, I thought. A piece that could reflect on travel, use its particular dissociation, and at the same time honor the spirit of the master: I would make a series of deft segues between my situation, whatever it turned out to be, and some of the great travel moments of Bellow's own protagonists—Herzog en route to Martha's Vineyard, Charlie Citrine hunkered down in a *pensión* in Madrid, Dean Corde behind the Iron Curtain—not just to pursue the obvious tactic of parallelism, but because Bellow was, among so many other things, a brilliant reflective scene maker who knew how to use the physical displacement of his characters to create an existential metaphysics. I mean, who else would write as Bellow did in *Humboldt's Gift,* apropos of a transatlantic flight: "The stewardess served whisky and Hawaiian macadamia nuts. We plunged across the longitudinal lines of the planet, this deep place that I was learning to think of as the great school of souls, the material seat of the spirit"? The idea had legs—all I had to do was make the connections.

This turned out to be the thing that would not and would not happen, not in frenetic Rome, where we stayed our first three days, but also not in the town of Civita di Bagnoregio, where we lived in idyllic seclusion for nearly two weeks, and where ideas might have been expected to flourish. I just could not find my path to Bellow. Put what English I would on my thoughts, they bent away from the subject. The primary evidence of things in front of me, things as they *are*, was at every moment just too strong, too strange. I could not get myself thinking in the usual way.

Winding back, I have never accepted flying, the premise of moving a huge congregation of people through space at impossible velocity and unthinkable height. Forget Bellow's plunging across lines of longitude: I was so deep in the plane—center bleachers, rear—that I couldn't even see out the window. What I had instead was the all-purpose miniscreen, the progress map on channel 1 that marked our movement across the Atlantic, "whale-road" of the kenners, with a slow nudging of dots writing out our vital statistics: putting us thirty-eight thousand feet over the water and contradicting our seeming immobility with the fact that we were cleaving the upper air at more than six hundred miles per hour. Is there a right way to think about this? Or to ponder the image of myself a few hours later, still awake, captive with my family in an Italian transport van, bumping and jittering past wildly picturesque ruins with the constant "what's that?" feeling that afflicts all travelers in Rome, as if anything that still holds some shape after two millennia has to be worthy of attention?

But Rome overwhelmed that preciosity fairly quickly. Before we'd even reached our hotel on the Via Turati, the gawking reflex had begun to subside. The Forum, the columns, the Colosseum off to the right like half a gigantic decaying set of dentures . . . We acceded to the sudden spectacle of history as readily as we had accepted the thrust of those turbines—but instead of a progress screen we now had our guidebooks, already open to the general map, the forefinger tracing the way past the icon of Santa Maria Maggiore, "built in, let's see, when was it?"

Where had I gotten the idea that I would brood calmly on the spirit of Bellow, the man who himself spent so much time just marking the path of his perplexity—at our imponderable presence in the murky bogs of being, at the radiant but finally illegible signs surrounding us on every side? Thinking could find no purchase. On our first full day in Rome my son, Liam, and I went back to our room for an afternoon rest, and when he flipped on the TV to look for Italian cartoons, we were hit instead by urgent flash images of rubble, maps and arrows, and talking Italian heads with their breakneck word chains: "terroristi . . . Londra . . . G-8 . . . Tony Blair . . . i morti . . ." There followed my own anxious groping for some sense of scale, of context, with the inevitable associative triggerings to 9/11, which for the rest of our lives will be the template sensation of apocalypse, of the absolute unreal.

Liam and I sat together on the bed, flicking between channels, using the redundancies of transmitted images to create the basic contours of what had happened, picking more and more recurrent words from the looping reportage. Once again I was addressing a map, now looking to bridge the distance with imagined sensation—what such chaos must feel like—as well as with long-ago memories of London (I'd roamed there far and wide as a drifting would-be expat in the summer of 1970). But I was on edge, unable to connect, really, even as I believed I ought to, the feeling of a gap sharpened by the presence of my son, who of course imagined that as a grown-up I understood all these codes and implications.

I'm not about to recount the blow-by-blow of our passage through what has to be one of the most touristed patches of the planet, except—except—insofar as certain moments seem to have had direct bearing on my failure to generate the valedictory thoughts I wanted. I'll say nothing at all of our long days in the tiny town of Civita, where the hours chased one another clockless and mostly cloudless outside our open windows and lazy inwardness held court. I could not have begun to put together a thought on Bellow then. It was all I could do to monitor the light twitching of the vines attached to every rough stone surface, or hold my gaze on one of the little green lizards stop-starting along the terrace wall. No, the object of my intended contemplation fell victim to the mind's overpowering need to replenish itself in looking. I could have stared at a web of fractured masonry all afternoon—possibly I did.

It was when we threw ourselves back into cities that I felt the man draw in closer, when, for instance, we stood outside the Colosseum looking for a point of entry and my wife, Lynn, was taken in by a grade B huckster from central casting, a louche-looking character in a cheap gladiator's costume who got the kids posing with him while she readied her camera, and who, we realized later when we looked at the photo, didn't even bother to toss away his cigarette for the shot; who somehow commandeered *five* euros from us for the privilege and left us gaping in his wake. I could imagine the master winking just then, for who was more attuned than Bellow to the poetry of the artful con?

Or on another day, as we first found our way into St. Peter's and felt the vertical lift of so much sculptured space, having to push down our amazement by degrees so that we could stand with a dozen others in front of Michelangelo's Pietà, its sorrow still sharply alive in spite of the cordon, the several centimeters of bulletproof Plexiglas and the chittering of digital cameras on all sides. I thought, though only fleetingly, of Bellow. He had lost his own mother very early; he would have seen past the legends and the Catholicism here. He would have found the balance of suffering and faith—the inward focus of Mary's turned-away face somehow pressing back against the world-heavy immobility of the body—I'm sure of it.

A few hours later I conjured him again, if only as a corroborating presence, when we all moved like members of some procession of the damned through halls and rooms en route to the Sistine Chapel, the tour leaders in front and behind holding high their colored paddles and insignias, marking every increment of progress with canned statistics and anecdotes, the swarms parting and then re-forming around us, while on every side and above, crammed to an unprecedented thickness of reference, glowed the treasures: the Raphaels, Signorellis, Ghirlandaios . . . And we all believed that their barely conned radiance was just a prelude, a kind of spirit ramp leading us all into the hallowed chamber, the elongated space of the chapel itself, where, higher than I could distinguish without constantly tilting my glasses, the signature treasure of Western culture was enshrined. The finger of God the patriarch was right then more familiar than any product logo, and the panels on every side of it looked to me, maybe to all of us, like a sheet of postal commemoratives. And every minute or so, almost as if timed, one or another of the guards would let out an explosive "Shhhh!" whereupon the huge buzz of the crowd would diminish for an instant before it built right back. Bellow would have loved that; he would have written it into a novel. And he would have, I'm sure, at some point looked away from the treasures above, worked his sharp eye through the room, inventorying the faces, caricaturing telltale nuances of character much as da Vinci might have, but also, good Balzacian, quietly pricing the watches and bracelets.

In that one sense then, yes, Bellow was with me, zooming in and out, shadowing my thoughts almost playfully, never quite taking on the heft of an actual idea, but in range, there. Except for one occasion, that is, a moment that back then was embedded in the long sequence of traveling days but that now, filtered through retrospect—through writing—looks to be the connection I was after.

We had gone to Florence, driving our rental car against all smart advice right into the teeth of the midsummer madness. For the kids, we said. Mainly. But for ourselves, too. After all, we were staying just two hours away, how could we not? Surely it couldn't be *that*— And then there we stood, our dazed little gang of four, smack in the middle of the Ponte Vecchio, turned into molasses by the terrorism of crowds, unable to move except by determined assault, watching those colored paddles and banners (the new tourist universal) bobbing up and down in a foreshortened vista of what looked like a mainly white Calcutta. At the same time, the hyper-real picturesque crushed at us from every side—the wide elbow of the Arno, with its bridges and tight hedging of facades, the Tuscan hills in the distance, the Giotto campanile off to the right, and behind it all the suspicion that some ancient auratic magnificence was waiting, just barely out of reach.

But we couldn't make the effort then. We were overwhelmed and we buckled, opting for a hasty circuit of immediate highlights, a meal, and a race back to the shady space of the *pensione.* But as the afternoon and evening wore on, I found that I couldn't quite let go of the inkling. I felt that I wanted connection, the rough nap of the real, and without telling anyone I set my mind on waking early. I mean "set" quite literally. I am blessed with almost completely reliable autosuggestion, so that when the very first dawn arrived, though our room was shuttered, I was up. Tiptoeing, carrying my sandals.

And indeed, I was for a good long time the only person abroad on the streets of Florence. Day was not yet official. I moved with a sense of entitlement, purposeful but slow, down the long main drag, across the now-deserted Ponte Vecchio, halting there long enough to savor in solitude the edging of light along the rooflines, then continuing on, without plan, turning right to bypass the Uffizi, following the dice roll of the streets, the lure of dim prospects, the lay of the shadows. And I went on this way for I don't know how long, at least an hour, until I began to feel the deep hankering for coffee—latte straight up in a no-nonsense glass. But I saw no open grates, no bars—it was just six—so at last I began to arc my way back toward what I knew was the center, the area with all the sights, everything we had ended up avoiding yesterday.

There is the rhythm, the physics, of walking, the drumbeat of repetition, stride, stride, stride, and then there is the fugue of the walking mind, laid over it, always different, always tied in some way to the panning of the gaze and the eye's quirky meandering, but possessing a music, an obsessive hum of its own, maybe related to the dreams of the night before, or a branch of association from some unexpected clue, a poster for a concert, a line from some old song, the smirky movements of a cat in a doorway. Thoughts advance with a private logic, follow their mysterious and inescapable track. And so it was on this morning—Florence, silence, the aura of all that broken-in beauty, the half-remembered Dante, and the message of time seeping through at every turn. Here was the far-gone bygone living on in the wakening modern light, so much past pressed down into these flat cobbled stones—such density and mass. And my mind just kept moving, floating abstractedly between the then and now, suspended, not so much forming thoughts as idly weighing contrasts—old world, new world—but at the same time hoping that with enough of this back-and-forth I might snatch some new reckoning for my own life. *Ticktock.* What could this predictable swing of mind and sense finally generate? Was there anything to be won beyond the walker's fine adrenaline?

It turns out that there was. Something *did* come to me near the end of this long ramble: in the space of a few strides, between one street corner and another, I found myself rushed by what I can only call a violence of clear feeling. An "epiphany"? Whatever it was, the detonating image came at me almost cinematically—I had an eyeblink flash of something very big rising up as if through deep water. Now, after, I can break the moment into a sequence. I was on a narrow street, heading back toward my side of the river, traversing a shadowy intersection, when I registered a kind of throb in my peripheral vision. More sensed than seen, but I saw it, too: a building. I stopped where I was. What thing made of stone could still unsettle the eye in a city like this—after the Pitti Palace, the campanile, the Baptistry? I took a few steps forward. And there it was, square in front of me: squat, primal, rigid in its own unlikely scale, a construction massive and palpably thick at the bottom, then slowly building up to a dome. But not just one of a thousand other Italian domes: this one felt in some vital way connected to the original shape of things. Opening night: a full thrust back into inspiration and the work of hands that made it real. Soon enough I would get my map and figure out that it was Brunelleschi's famous Rotunda, but for that one moment I saw it unnamed—and it filled my looking right up.

The timing could not have been better—I understand that now. My thoughts were already primed. All that walking and looking: I had by stages come around to the question of religion, realizing in my slow way that faith and beauty had at some point long ago first come together, and that that special power of seeing had then moved through Italy, through Europe. Now I was asking—it was impossible not to— if we still had, in our own late world, any larger measure of art, any real sense of lastingness, or greatness. Not like this, no. I was sure of that. I was, I know, just a few quick beats away from taking up the question of the word, the book, the survival of writing. And if I had I would without question have called on the shade of Bellow once again—for help with a

As Above: Saul Bellow
127

mental frame to hold it all, but also for solace, affirmation that the large view was still possible, or had been until very recently. That's how my thinking moves. But though I didn't invoke him then, my reverie didn't just vaporize either. It stayed with me through the rest of the trip, gradually mingling with all my thoughts of him, his sense of the soul always alive behind the maps and charts and labels, his enormous unquenched delight in the whole chaos of the human, until I got it—of course: I'd been thinking of him all along.

What Do *You* Do for Work, Daddy?

Though it never happened exactly like this, it might well have: Liam or Mara sitting with me on the front step in the afternoon, watching as the neighbors come home from their jobs—Dave Allard with his big welding truck, John Hickman hurrying right past us on his walkway in a straight-looking suit, briefcase in hand, Marie across the street in her clean car and office clothes—and as I make the imagined camera pan full circle around to the big man sitting there in his jeans and T-shirt, barefoot, I hear the obvious indicting question: "What do *you* do for work, Daddy?" Of course, I pause before answering, create my defensive cloud of self-irony. What do I say? The easiest answer, the one I give to people in need of some reassurance, is that I teach. Some of them do wonder, I know. My hours and clothes are different. I work at home, I say. I take a lot of time to prepare classes and grade papers. That usually satisfies whoever is asking. And depending on my mood and my energy, it's what I probably would tell—and have told—my kids when they looked at me in that way, wanting to understand not just what I did but also, in a deeper way, who we were. Alas, my answer doesn't begin to satisfy me, though my life would be much simpler if it did. For me teaching is an add-on or, better, an off-shoot, something that both taketh away and giveth. It draws energy from the main thing, the writing, though it supposedly then compensates me by buying time and making the writing possible. And while it's true that a certain number of hours a week—mental hours, I mean—are given over to thinking and worrying about the teaching I do, I don't count those as part of my legitimate work. In fact, I barely even count as legitimate the hours spent conducting classes or meeting with students or grading papers. I don't write them off as waste, of course, but they're not the real work. Whether I fill them matter-of-factly or with inspired associative flights, my core sense of self-worth is unaffected. The only thing that matters in that other—real—economy is whether I feel I have put together words in a way that means something to me; whether I have advanced my private cause of writing. On this one score I am impossibly harsh and un-forgiving, impervious to any excuses or arguments about mitigating fac-tors. Either I am writing—in the deeper sense of the word—or I'm not. I want to pause on this distinction, for to say that I have worked at putting words on paper is not the same as saying I am "writing." In fact, there is a world of difference. The participle is everything. To be writing is to be in a particular relation to the world; it is to be linguistically in process, not waiting for a wave but engaging it, instincts and reflexes on high alert, whereas simply fulfilling the outer demand to be putting words on a page toward some intended end is never more than waiting for that wave. The former redeems. The latter, merely dutiful, hopes for redemption, and when redemption won't come feels its possibility mocked. "What do *you* do for work, Daddy?" Honest answer? I wait for signs, for the faraway shift of the surface water that signals the approaching wave. But I can't say that to anyone, except maybe another writer. Any sane person would want to know, "Where's the work in that?" And I wonder, too. Is it in the waiting, getting into the right responsive condition? Or is it in whatever happens when things finally click? Both, of course. Though they are not to be compared.

I often imagine the cinema verité version of the writer at his desk. Like Andy Warhol's *Blow Job,* it would be a film centered on an essentially expressionless face. The writer's gaze, like that of the oral beneficiary, is turned around inward, with all concentration being directed to a very specific end. Even the most intuitive and sympathetic cinematographer would have to scramble to find the occasions of drama, catch the mo-ment when the fuse inside the fingers suddenly burned down and released an explosion—words, words, words—and then initiated the madden-ing irregular stop/start of composition. His close-up shots would work to convey the tension that underlies this special act of expression, the cam-era zooming in on the outer cues, fingers hovering over the keyboard, a thumb and forefinger pinching the mustache hairs right below the nos-trils, the mike picking up the sound of a slowly indrawn breath, then maybe another flurry of typing. These bits are as close as the film could get to what happens inside, which is not—for me at least—any orderly sort of voice-over dictation, but more like a slow garbled churning of word sounds with the keyed-up, tensely auditory self listening for combinations, willing them, searching for the best way to get at the basic line of sense, looking to find the saying that tells me only in that moment a vital part of what I'm after, the actual expression. "What do you do for your work?" If I'm honest: this. I go way deep inside myself, though who will accept that as an answer? But it's real—it matters more than anything. And how well it has gone minute by minute, and sentence by sentence, has everything to do with the rest of my day, whether I carry grocery bags to the car with a light or heavy step, whether I can make myself stand face-to-face with people in conversation, whether I hum when I walk around the block. But again, which part is the work? Is it in the typing or writing of words, or in that strange suspended listening that doubles as thinking? Or is it in whatever I do—and I don't even know what that is—to get myself into a mood that has to be there for the listening to happen? And what is that work in relation to the rest of life? Who knows? But the answer starts with the sense I get, when I put my writing away and stand up, of having traveled somewhere very far, to someplace where they use different currencies, where the water swirls counterclockwise down the drain. If I have been working in public, hunched over a table in my neighborhood Starbucks, I very often move back into the day like an astronaut stepping out of an antigravity chamber. Everything seems strange. My car is a Claes Oldenburg sculpture of a car; those people walking by on the sidewalk are character actors hired to play people I might see in my town. I have to buy vegetables on the way home, but all I want to do is roll down the window and have a cigarette, because the smoke so nicely eases the ache of strangeness, filling the terrible vacuum between there and here. It joins things, makes a filmy stitch between the nothing and the something. But since Daddy mainly hides what he does all day—because he can't find the words to say it—Daddy hides this, too.

131

Every Day

Every day driving home from work I stop at the long red light on Memorial Drive at River Street, and every day the same thin man appears patrolling the space between the two lanes of northbound traffic. He carries a jar and a sign asking for money. He is not the only person with a sign along my route—there are usually several others who work the lights near the Alewife T stop, but that is a fast-changing population, whereas the River Street man has been there for many seasons now. I expect to see him as I come up the stretch past the Trader Joe's, and I do. If he's not pacing along between the cars, then he is standing under the tree on the right-hand corner of the intersection. He has long since figured out the intervals of the light, when to step in, when to hang back. And of course sometimes he just takes a break, holds still looking toward the river. He is handsome in a thin-faced way, middle-aged, perfectly without expression. I should be able to describe his sign, his jar, and how he is dressed, but I can't, not past the point of the generic. The sign asks for money for food, the jar is plastic, and the clothing is nondescript workingman's clothing. My vagueness might suggest that I don't see him, and in some ways perhaps I don't—it seems rude to stare or study. But I am very much aware of him, the way he holds himself—straight and tall—and how, also polite, he never looks at the person he is approaching, but always farther on, whether at the next car, or beyond, at the line backing up, or maybe he's not focusing on anything in particular, just looking out. But he is clearly reading the cues around him, for I also notice how quickly he can break stride and bend down when he sees someone rummaging in a purse or, if it's me, looking over to fish for change in the car's cup well. Then he will pause and bring his head into range of the window, but hesitantly, tactfully, never giving the impression that he is eager, or conveying disappointment if it turns out I have nothing to give. His manners, if that's what they are, are perfect. Every time I have disappointed him he has found a way to get me off the hook, to thank me for looking. When I straighten up I already see his back in my side-view mirror. And when the light changes I notice that he has made his way back over to the verge.

I don't always give the man money. In fact, often I don't, even when I have change in the well. I'm not sure I can explain how my impulses run—the impulse to ignore his asking, the impulse to give him something. My actions aren't based on any judgment I have about his need, though I do, naturally, wonder how much he takes in and what he does with it. I don't think he spends it on alcohol. He has, if anything, the air of a former drinker. Besides, if drink were the problem, it would be hard for him to work the light every day like this. Whatever it is that brings him here is deep and sorrowful, and my idle guessing does not touch it. As he patrols the lane between our idling cars, his world moves past ours, ours past his. It's more than I can fathom.

Many times I wait out the light without engaging; I stare straight ahead. I can do this, I tell myself, because I have given and will give again. I even imagine that the man recognizes me and understands. For there are just times when I actively do *not* wish to give. I'm stuck in some righteousness or refusal and don't have any impulse to battle it. I can wait him out for days on end in just this state. But then, who knows why, something changes—I can feel the shift even when I'm still at a distance. I see his silhouette way up ahead and already I'm tilting forward to see if I have change in my cup holder, or else I'm fishing my wallet from my front pocket. I want to give him something. I'm impatient to reach the light and impatient for him to come up alongside my car. What is this? Many things at once: a surge of human decency, a short-lived awakening to economic injustice, a recognition of "there but for fortune . . ." But also—more selfishly—I find a superstitious wagering impulse, as if my little kindness will be repaid in another form, or will at least replenish the account—my conscience—that has evidently been exhausted of whatever credit I earned with my last token offering.

Starbucks

One of the regulars in my life, out on the far periphery but there none-theless, is the dowdy, garishly made-up, bag-toting older woman whom I see regularly at my neighborhood Starbucks. She likes to sit at one of the tables by the big street-facing window, with her various parcels arrayed by her feet, and a newspaper messily spread out all over the tabletop. She bends over and reads—a big to-do somehow—but makes it a point to look up whenever someone steps into her radius, which seems considerable to me. As often as not, she will greet the person—she seems to know quite a few of the people who come in—or else she will loudly remark on the weather or on what the person is holding, announcing the title of a book in hand or endorsing the pastry selection. For a long time she irritated me beyond belief. If I spotted her there at her table as I was coming along the sidewalk my heart would sink, and as soon as I entered I would quickly scan for a seat as far as possible from where she sat. Sometimes, though, only one of the other small window tables would be free and I would fume over my book or notebook, not even quite sure what was making me so irritated. "Everything!" I would maybe say if someone asked, but of course the subject never came up. I was irked by the look of her, the need she had to create chaos around herself; the indiscriminate opportunism—promiscuity—of her way of hailing and trying to engage whoever stepped into her range. She even made a try at me once, asked me if I was going to do the crossword puzzle in the paper I was carrying (I was), but I was so curt, moved on so quickly, that she didn't strike again. I suppose it was her apparent lack of pride, of boundaries, that got to me—that and the suspicion that underneath the fuss and bluster was another human abyss.

Which ought to have pushed me toward kindness and fellow feeling, but for whatever reason didn't. When I ended up sitting close to her, and she fell into one of her grating interchanges with a person walking past, I would catch myself actively grimacing, making faces at her back, or else sharply shaking my head, as if by doing that enough I could hurl her presence away.

This ritual of lowercase loathing continued for the longest time, until it became familiar. Eventually I was more bemused than bothered. Then one afternoon I was sitting on the other side of the café, in one of the comfortable armchairs they used to have, reading. The woman had walked past me on her way in, I had noted her bags and clutter, and if I heard her saying something to a customer I'm sure I gave a small ritual headshake. But my attention that day was directed at a tall, serious-looking man sitting in the armchair opposite mine. Recognizing him as another longtime regular, I tried to make out what he was so absorbed in reading, couldn't quite, and then, losing interest, turned back to my own book, only every now and then looking over to frame him in a general contemplation.

I find I do this all the time, simply fix my eyes on some person in my vicinity—he (or she) has to be oblivious of me—and take him in. Not to any special purpose: I am not trying to guess a secret. I just absorb the person's presence, his human sculptural solidity, as if to say, "This, *this* is another human being!" I look at his clothes, see if he is wearing jewelry, focus in on his face, his expression, as he drinks coffee, or eats, or just stares into the distance. I do this mainly with people who are by themselves. I cannot get to the point of contemplation if I'm sitting by two people who are talking. Though then I will listen avidly to their conversation, tuning in especially to their inflections and repetitions and the rhythm of their exchange.

On this one afternoon, though, I was mainly reading my book, checking in obliquely from time to time on the man opposite, when suddenly I realized that the woman was at his side. They were talking—I hadn't heard them begin—familiar, involved, carrying on what seemed to be an old conversation. We were in election season and they were talking politics. The terms and references were clear to both of them. I don't remember any specific thing they said, but I was struck, sharply struck, by the informed level of the to-and-fro. Everything the man said, and everything the woman said, showed them to be nuanced and opinionated observers of the political scene. And they went on this way for some minutes. I suspended my reading completely, though of course I kept the book in front of my face. I wasn't listening to their points, or weighing their assertions—I didn't know enough to be weighing. Rather, I was recalibrating, revolutionizing my whole conception of the dowdy woman, going through all of my earlier impressions in the light of what was now obvious: that she was intelligent, articulate, and—this became clear as I listened—full of feisty independence. Listening, I found myself taking the greatest pleasure in her words, her way of speaking, even the nasal tone that before had had me baring my teeth over my notebook. After she left, I glanced again at the man opposite. He had receded back into his reading.

That was a year ago. I still go for coffee almost every day. I see the woman several times a week without fail. I saw her this afternoon. I'm still not at ease with her manner and still find ways to hurry past her when I have to. Not that she makes any more overtures. She sees me there, but says nothing. She took my measure far more accurately than I took hers.

Coffee

I was having lunch the other day with G., an acquaintance, in a coffee shop in Harvard Square. G. is someone I haven't seen in quite some time, so not only was there a good deal of basic catching-up to be done, but we needed to relocate whatever slippery frequency there was between us that made the right kind of conversation possible. G. and I don't know each other well, but we've had a few exchanges over the years that have shown us we can get past the niceties and find the threads that lead us some-where; we can zero in on mutual passions and then stay with them atten-tively enough that when we're both ready to push back our chairs, we feel that we have gained on something, that with enough time we really could be friends. Though to be honest I think we are both now old enough to know how hard it is to move from this episodically promising condition to whatever it is we now call friendship. And how many of my relationships fall into this category? Many, many. Could it be I am not really looking for any more deeper involvements? Somehow these thoughts are with me here at the table, though not in any coherent way. Rather, they are part of the feeling that decides how far to push things, how intimate to get, whether to volunteer or solicit confidences that I might not with another person. G. is a writer, quick with words and able to give his expressions that little torquing spin, that fillip that always extends a promise of "more." He has an independent mind—is, in fact, finishing a book on silence. But he is not one to come forward except by small degrees. The questions are always *how much?* and *how far?* I study him now, catching his eye when he talks, but also alighting again and again on the freshly shaven area just above the thin roué's mustache he wears with his beard. He has trimmed the mustache exactly like this for the ten or so years I've known him—it was the very first thing about him that I noticed. And as we talk I am won-dering, in that way I do, just how he goes about shaving that narrow little area just below the nostril; it seems a feat, an exertion, one that asks—this is how my mind works—a daily faith in life, an ability to answer the "why bother?" question enough to keep performing such a delicate operation. We talk about his project for a while. It intrigues me, and I find all kinds of ideas and references coming to mind. But I also know that he is mostly finished with the work, past wanting suggestions—is, in fact, probably at the point where recommendations are more irritation than incitement. I can tell this by the way he lets things drop, how he nods when I offer a thought but then does not pick it up. He is done with his book on silence. And me? My work? Well—I decide to be honest, to nudge that counter a bit—I confide to G. that the writing has been more difficult for me recently, that I can't seem to do the dutiful expository thing the way I used to; I find myself resisting, being willful. G. is paying attention, I feel it. It could be that he goes through his own writerly struggles. I wonder—again, it's not a full thought, something more like a mental grimace—whether my admitting this in any way exposes a flank. Does it somehow lower me in his eyes? Do I feel the slightest deflation in the mood between us, or am I just projecting my own anxiety? I pause, hold for a beat.

It is here, midconversation, midlull, as I'm looking for some little cue of gesture or expression that would tell me to say more, or else cut my confession short, that something compels me to glance over to the table at my left, just behind G.'s shoulder. As I do I catch the eye of a well-dressed, clean-shaven man—an anomaly in this faux-bohemian café—who turns quickly away. He is sitting by himself, very close to us really. Something about that action, his bearing, the vibration that comes from his direction, tells me that he has been listening. Not just in the way of overhearing—I don't think I've been exactly broadcasting my writerly woes—but *listening*, tuning in and following. And with this realization, the whole nature of my conversation changes. I feel it happening, like when you see a movie screen splitting neatly in half. All of a sudden I am not just having an interchange with G., I'm also imagining it from the vantage of the man at the next table. Who are we? How do we look? How do we sound? Two bearded men, bookish looking, careful with their words. I don't know why I should care, but for some reason I can't turn off this monitoring. I feel the performing self stir to life as I talk. Whereas before I directed my words just to G., and responded to him alone, now each gesture and expression is automatically weighed for its effect. How will they seem to the well-dressed man? What story is he assembling? Nor does it end here. I find myself imagining, who knows why—narcissistic projection maybe—that he is listening not just because he is interested but because he is himself a writer. In fact, I'm sure of it. We had only a split-second meeting of the eyes, but I saw it all.

And now my midday coffee with my "friend" has turned into something else. Because I don't know the other man, because I imagine as I do, he becomes the more important listener. G. is nodding, asking, filling in my blanks with the encouragements that allow a conversation to move forward. But the well-dressed man behind him—who has not, by the way, looked over since, which only confirms my every suspicion—has the power to judge and absolve. By listening and comprehending he can fix the problem. Which, if I may return to it, is the deepest problem that can afflict a writer—the problem of will, of desire, of *faith*. Faith, in humankind, in the value and purpose of the whole business. I go on, laying out my recent doubts for G., elaborating more than I might have before I caught the listener's eye, and as I do it seems to me that I am gaining on it. This is not mere human insufficiency that is being exposed, it is also something philosophical, something almost noble. To my secret auditor I set out my case. I am very careful now to underscore the profundity of my hesitations and vacillations. Of course he says nothing, gives no sign. He wouldn't. I see just the top of his head as he bends over his plate. But he is listening. Even as we switch subjects and bring our coffee to a close, he is still tuning us in. And I feel as I gesture to the waiter for the check that something has shifted for me. I know as G. and I push back our chairs and leave together that he, the well-dressed man now looking deliberately into the middle distance, has grasped my situation in its every nuance and is thinking about it.

Magda

You maybe don't remember all of this little episode, my friend, but I'm guessing you do: some things adhere even if others don't, and I'm putting my money on what the French call *amour-propre,* my theory being that anything connected with *that* is not likely to slip through the meshes, which we both agree seem to get larger as time goes on. Writing even this far I realize that while a sentence is meant to be a retrieval system, a preservative, its dynamics can also spawn the branching paths that take us, step by step, away from our intended destination. And I have one, a destination, yes. It is the capture of a moment that now gets me smiling every time I think of it, so that—bringing in the mail, say, or waiting for someone to pass me the salt—I will recall the picture and feel my face suddenly creasing up, causing anyone who knows me to say, "*What* is so funny?" To which I want to say *never mind,* but no, here it is, though you have to bear in mind that my reluctance has everything to do with having to backtrack enough to make the context sufficiently clear for the nuance to come through—at least some of it, perfect transmission, of course, requiring complete knowledge of both parties (you, me) and the history of our conversations. But here it is. It was a few weeks back and I had stopped off in Amherst for our long-overdue visit. I don't have to say "You may recall," because of course you do. In fact, you recall almost everything to a scary degree—which as you'll see is also, psychologically speaking, part of the context. Anyway, we had agreed to meet at Amherst Books, where we have several times met in the past, bookstores being perfect docking sites for bookish fellows like us, who first met in a bookstore twenty-some years ago, when I was working the counter and you were in grad school across the street and a daily browser, one of our "cormorants"—the tag is from Coleridge, I think, and of course you could correct or corroborate me in a second. Which I hasten to say is not irrelevant either, because one of the really enjoyable parts of our getting to know each other better, later, when I drove in to teach at Mount Holyoke and we had lunch every week—for *years*—was our nonstop game of lobbing well-known literary tags at each other, which quite early on started our fantasy of compiling a compendium, an updated and slightly recast version of Flaubert's *Dictionary of Received Ideas,* to include all the nuggets of lore that English Department types have been using as conversation fodder for the past half century, such as, Balzac *survived by eating pigeons he caught outside his garret window,* and Malcolm Lowry *arrived in America to see Conrad Aiken with only a boot and a copy of* Moby-Dick *in his suitcase.* That sort of thing. Which is necessary to this account, too, because without it there would be no understanding the tone and tenor of our chatter as we walked down the hill from whatever quadrangle that was and across the playing fields of the college. But we haven't gotten that far yet. I'm still back in the bookstore, browsing and waiting for you to arrive and clap me on the back, which you do pretty much right on schedule. "*Good* to see you!" you boom, and I boom back, "Good to see *you!*" And we then linger around the display tables, pointing at this or that new book, or fatuous blurb, until you finally say, "Hey—" and drag me over to a table near the back of the store, where you introduce me to a man—of course you know everyone in town—whose name I now forget, and whom I profess to be delighted to meet, until he quips, with no evident malice, that we've had this pleasure "seven or eight times now," which I know to be an exaggeration, but that hardly salves my barely concealed mortification, for this, exactly this, is what, I will tell you a few minutes later, the "story of my life" is, this forgetting of faces and names. And you will be friend enough to laugh—we are crossing the street outside the store—instantly placing it into perspective. Do you also allow that you do it all the time yourself, or am I getting ahead of myself?

Never mind. We start off walking, catching up, talking about your writer friend who has just taken an appointment at the college, and—how literary this all is—running into another of your friends, the well-known older critic, who is walking his dog at the far side of that quadrangle, the name of which I ought to know, since I did teach in that very building there for a whole semester some years ago. But never mind. Your friend the well-known older critic—with whom I have never been at ease, not since I criticized a biography he wrote eons ago and received his withering note in the mail almost instantly—does a perfect imitation of patrician inattentiveness as we stand together for a moment on the walkway. But just for a moment. Soon enough we are off, down the hill to the fields, picking up this theme and that, more threads in play even since our encounter with the critic, though we have not yet located, as we always at some point do, the master theme, that one reference to which almost every conversational digression somehow returns. But there's time enough. Have I remarked on the weather, the near-perfect October afternoon, the sun already dropped behind the trees over there, beyond which—"That way, a mile or so"—is the house you've just bought and will be moving to in a few months, and just behind which, you point out, are the railroad tracks, informing me, you who remember everything, that Emily Dickinson's father had a locomotive named after him, and . . . ? Well, we're on to talk about our children now, what they do in school, and then more generally youth—*Pass the bottle!*

And as we go up the hill back toward town, there is no question but that we need to go get a cup of coffee at Rao's. And yes, here we go, getting to the point, but also, I think, to the day's master theme—at least it now has that status in *my* mind. We've come down the block on the main drag of Amherst, have turned right onto that little sidewalk leading to the café, which is set back some way from the street, and just as I'm suggesting that we take an outdoor table—because it really is a spectacular afternoon—someone calls out your name. Jubilantly, I would say—one excited syllable—and we both stop. You turn to your right and extend your arms wide (you are nothing if not full of bonhomie, *bonhomie*), and into them steps a very attractive woman who is speaking with what sounds to me like some kind of Eastern European accent, and after your long hug, which I find myself acutely envying, she steps free and fixes me with a knowing smile, indeed a *very* knowing smile, a smile of the sort that convinces me that of course she and I have met, too, have probably even talked at length. It would have been years ago, of course.

Back when I came to town, I met many people, went to readings and a few parties, and so to me that look can only mean that we know each other and that she is waiting for the recognition to arrive, though she is also willing to extend a slight bit of credit. And then—slowly, confidently, warmly—this attractive woman of Eastern European extraction holds out her hand and I take it in mine, shaking it once or twice, smiling, shaking it again, more slowly now as it becomes clear that she is not letting go, and we stand together, the three of us, under the perfect translucent dome created by this contact, smiling, staring at each other, me intent on giving nothing away as I ransack every last memory catalog, desperate to stumble upon the unambiguous verifying bit that will allow me to say a name, or even just cite an occasion, something, *anything*. But before that can happen our hand-holding eternity, our moment of perfect timelessness, crumples in upon itself and she says, almost triumphantly, as if she herself had only just now remembered it: "Magda." Magda. And then right away I hear those two syllables echoed—in loud corroboration—by you, and as Magda lets go of my hand, leaving me completely unmoored—*Have we met? Am I once again being rude?*—you move into the breach. "Magda is doing work on Emily Dickinson," you say, as easy and confident as can be. I nod. I content myself with listening and smiling, trying to convince myself that if I have failed again, it has been forgiven, paved over. But the issue continues to nag as I stand there; it eats into the pleasure I've been taking in the afternoon, and when the two of you at last finish your to-and-fro, after Magda has gone up on tiptoe to kiss you on the cheek and smiled at me and started walking off toward the street, I prepare to confide this newest mortification. Before that happens, though, before anything, you are shaking your head, leaning toward me confidingly, saying, "God, that was embarrassing!" I assume you mean my idiotic blankness, the second of the day. But no. You're laughing now, that same laugh you laughed when we were leaving the bookstore. "I could *not* think of her name," you say. "Not for the life of me, and I *know* her—the whole time she was holding your hand there she was waiting. She was testing me. Did you catch that? Magda. Magda, Magda, Magda." "Magda," I echo back, "Mag-da. Who could forget a name like Magda?" Indeed, I've wondered this a few times these past weeks—bending over to test the temperature of the water in the tub, raking up the last leaves out back, tracking the lit numbers on the elevator panel at work, 4-3-2-1—each time smiling that smile that's so hard to explain, though you can't say I haven't tried.

The Points of Sail

The nerve of fathering is woven through the moment—and here and now is the place to start. Late July 2008, Cape Cod. We have come down almost every summer for the past twenty years. This time we are staying in Truro, my wife, Lynn, our son, Liam, and his friend Caleb, and I. Our daughter, Mara, will take a few days off from her job next week to join us, arriving when Caleb leaves. There will be three days when we are all four together, the basic unit, taken for granted for so many years, but now become as rare as one of those planetary alignments or convergences that I no longer put stock in. *This,* though, I do put stock in. The thought of us all reassembled reaches me, wakes me with the strike of every blue ocean day.

It's midafternoon and I'm in Provincetown, sitting on a deck on the bayside, at one of those rental spots. Liam and Caleb have persuaded me to rent two Sunfish sailboats so they can sail the harbor together. Caleb has been taking sailing lessons all summer at home, and Liam had some a few years back, though as was clear as soon as they launched, ten minutes ago, he had forgotten whatever he had learned. As Caleb's boat arrowed out toward the horizon, Liam's sat turned around with sails luffing, and I watched his silhouette jerking the boom and tiller this way and that until at last he got himself repointed and under way. I was smiling, not worrying much about the wisdom of letting him out in his own boat—he's fourteen and as big as I am—though I did take note of a smudge of dark clouds moving in behind me.

Once Liam joined up with Caleb, the two little Sunfish zigged and zagged for the longest time in the open area between the long pier and the dozens of boats anchored in the harbor, and I fell into a kind of afternoon fugue watching them. The book I'd brought lay facedown on the little table where I sat. I tracked the movement of the boats and half-listened to two men behind me talking about the perils of gin and various hangover remedies, and every so often I stood up to stretch and to glance up at the sky. Shielding my eyes with my hand, I panned left along the shoreline, past the clutter of waterfront buildings and pilings, toward Truro and Wellfleet.

I don't remember what year we first started coming to the Cape regularly. We had been down once or twice for shorter visits before we had kids. Massachusetts was still new to us—Lynn and I are both Midwesterners—and going to the ocean felt like adventure, a splurge. Fresh seafood, bare feet in the brine. What a sweet jolt to the senses it all was. And isn't this one of the unexpected things about getting older: suddenly remembering not just the specifics of an event but also the original intensity, the *fact* of the original intensity?

Those first times have mostly slipped away, replaced—overruled—by the years and years, the layers and layers, of family visits. The place, which is to say the *places*—the many rental spots in Wellfleet and Truro, including some fairly grim-looking habitats—has become an archive of family life. Driving along Route 6 in either direction I have only to glance at a particular turnoff to think—or say out loud if Lynn is beside me—"that was the place with the marshy smell" or whatever tag best fits.

All of which is to say that this whole area, everything north of the Wellfleet line—which for me is marked by the Wellfleet Drive-In—is dense with anecdote. I have this mental storage box with its twenty-plus years of excerpts, all of them from summer, all from vacations away from our daily living and therefore of a kind, a time line separate from everything else. "That first summer we . . ." Except that memory does not obey time lines, but associations. Shake the photos in the box until they are completely pell-mell, then reach in. That dark path by the bayside rental fits right next to the place with the horses, and that fits next to the field where we threw Frisbees. Like that. When I shade my eyes and follow the shoreline, I am not so much seeing the things in front of me as pointing myself *back*. I am fanning the pages of a book I know, not really reading, just catching a phrase here, another there.

But now I turn again, I look across the tables on the deck, and over the railing, and out along the line described by the pier to my right. I see the two Sunfish, Caleb's with the darker sail heeling nicely into the wind, cutting toward the open water past pier's end; Liam's lagging, not quite right with the wind, but at least making headway. And I check over my shoulder to see how the clouds have gained, feeling a first tiny prick of anxiety. The boat rental people said the bay just past the pier was fine, but they also said they were a bit shorthanded today, that they wouldn't be taking their boat out quite as much to patrol. This flashes back to me as I see Caleb's boat slip out of sight behind the end of the pier, though I find that when I sit up straight I can follow the top part of his blue sail—accompanied, some distance behind, by Liam's, which is red.

We came those first summers when Mara was little, just the three of us, so often renting on a shoestring and ending up in some places that in retrospect seem rankly depressing, but then, when we were in them, were mainly fine. We ignored or joked about smells and bugs and cupboards lined with floral sticky paper and the molten-toned seascapes bolted to the walls. We took pride in "making do," and I think now that we had endless patience for the clattery busywork of being young parents, the stroller pushing, pretend playing, all the up and back repetitions. I remember one summer we set ourselves up in a box-shaped little house—it was one of a dozen or so—on a hillside near Wellfleet. And in our largesse, before ever even setting eyes on the place, we invited my mother to visit for a few days, with Lynn's sister to arrive as soon as she left. It turned out that there was barely room for all of us in the living room, with its huge picture window fronting the road. It rained most of the week. I was beside myself with boredom. But I also wanted to be a good father. I played and played with Mara, trying to make her vacation a happy one. Alas, we had nowhere to go. My only diversion was a box of dominoes found in the closet. I sat Mara down on the floor beside me and we built towers. Over and over, piece by ticking piece, always the same basic design. How high could we make it? And how irritated I got if Mara knocked one of my good towers down. I was building for myself, desperate to stay amused. Somewhere we have a Polaroid of the two of us sitting beside our prize construction. Looking at the photo, I think what a stunning, unbelievably sweet little girl she was—and how ridiculous it was for me to get so serious about stacking those bones.

What kind of father was I? I know that I tried to be different from my father, who all throughout my childhood maintained that he loved us—and clearly did—but who also told us, often, that we would appreciate him only when we were older and more intelligent. *Then* we would talk. But I could not imagine having that kind of detached deferral with my own child. I wanted entry to her world, a role in shaping her mind, her sense of things. I wanted to get as close as I could.

My problem was that I had no idea how to proceed. I was never one for playing. The sight of a spinner on a gussied-up board game or some molded plastic doll filled me with fatigue. I hated almost all toys, and I could not endure the infantilized pretend chatter that was the required accompaniment to all forms of parent-child play, at least from what I'd observed. "Snuffy is a *niiiiiice* kitty . . ." Yikes! I could finally do only what I knew to do, what I *liked* to do. I could talk. I invented characters, told stories, created plot situations that grew into one another and became more and more elaborate over time. Steffie and Kevin, their friend Lenny, the villains Moe and Joe, Steffie's rival Cherry Lalou—and the world they lived in, the street, neighborhood, town . . . I worked hard at these, the adventures were good ones—so I thought, anyway—full of surprises, resisting pat endings, but still upholding a basic picture of a moral universe, a triumph of idealism over low impulse. And Mara loved them. Every night, or whenever we had time together, she would beam at me: "Tell me a Kevin and Steffie, Dad." This went on for years.

Mara is almost twenty now. She is taking a break from college, living with roommates in an apartment in Belmont, ten minutes from where we live.

She has a forty-hour-a-week job in a stationery store in Harvard Square, though she barely makes ends meet. She is, by her own admission, unsettled, experiencing vivid and frightening dreams and moods that can suddenly plummet and leave her feeling sad and exposed. The sensations she describes are familiar to me—they reach all the way back into my own young years.

I wasn't thinking about Mara just then, as I stood up again to stretch on the deck, but I was very much aware of her. Her funks, the tone of her recent phone calls, knowing that she would be coming soon. I peered out at what I could see of the bay, but it was all there in my peripheral vision.

I was having my first real doubt now. I could still see the tips of both sails, moving toward the other part of the bay, just above the edge of the pier, clean little shark-fin shapes. But the sky was definitely darkening and the wind was picking up slightly and the farther out Liam took his boat, the less confidence I had in his bluster about knowing how to sail. I turned around to see if there was a clock in the rental shed. The girl who worked there had left her counter and was standing on a crate, shading her eyes and peering at the harbor. She must have picked up on my agitation because just then she said: "They'll be fine—but they shouldn't go too far out." I nodded. They would know that, I told myself. Then: They're fourteen-year-old boys, they *won't* know. I looked back quickly to make sure I saw the sails.

Liam has always been different from Mara. Six years younger, he is made from other material. While she is delicate, slightly wan, he is fleshy and boisterously solid. He always has been. Since preschool he has never not been the biggest boy in his class. Barely into his teens, he has already caught up to me, and I am not small. The other night I told him to stand up straight against a wooden beam in the Truro house. I put the top of a DVD case flat on his head and drew a faint line. Then I told him to do the same for me. We had to laugh—we were the thickness of a pencil lead apart.

Given his size and his point-blank confidence, I tend to forget his age and essential vulnerability. When I have to face it I can get overwhelmed. That he could hurt himself, cry a child's tears. Or be in danger. The worst was years ago. He was seven or eight years old, in summer camp. Lynn and I got a call at noon one day that we should come get him, that he was in the infirmary, having what appeared to be an asthma attack. We hurried over to bring him home, worried, but also thinking he had just overtaxed himself. We told him to rest in his room. Suddenly he was standing at the top of the stairs, red in the face, making a noise that was almost a bleat, terror on his face. He couldn't breathe, he was choking for air. There was not the slightest hesitation. We sat him down there on the top step and called the doctor, who told us to get an ambulance right away. Which we did. And moments later—time was a jumble—I was behind the wheel of our car, following an ambulance across town, hurtling through red lights, my calm life gone into a hyperventilating freefall that would only stop more than an hour later when a doctor came out to assure us that his breathing had been stabilized and that he would be fine.

How long it took—maybe years—for that shock to fully ebb, some trace of that anxiety not to be there every time he went outside to play, daily breathing treatments notwithstanding. I think of the way we look at our children when we are afraid, the way we read their eyes to see if they are telling us everything, and a terrible sense of their fragility, which for me goes all the way back to the very first night we brought Mara home from the hospital and set her up in a little crib. I remember how I just lay there listening to the breathing sounds, sure that if I tuned them out for an instant they would stop. A superstition, much as I used to believe that if I relaxed my will for an instant while flying, the airplane I was in would instantly plummet. Life has taught me about fear and about grandiose presumptions, but only gradually.

Liam and Mara, what a strange distribution of personalities—no, what a pairing of souls. I have to think in terms of souls where my closest people are concerned. To think of them as personalities diminishes them, a personality being something one can put a boundary around somehow. They could not be more different, in who they are, and in what each drew forth from us as parents. We never had a program or a plan. I have never had a clear instinct for what kind of father to be, not in terms of what I should be doing, modeling, instructing. I have somehow trusted to being myself. Maybe a better version—kinder, more attentive, and more consistent in my responses than I might be if I did not feel the responsibility of children.

My idea—and feeling—of being a father has changed from year to year, if not week to week. The father of a newborn is very different from the father of a toddler or a school-age child or a preteen or . . . Is there anything constant in it, besides the love and care, the great givens, the fact that I would do anything at any time to ensure their safety and well-being? But in terms of who I *am*—well, it stands to reason, doesn't it? The father of newborn Mara was thirty-six, the father of teenage Mara was fifty, and the man looking out for some trace of his teenage son is slowly pushing sixty.

I keep an image to orient myself, from an afternoon moment on a Wellfleet side road some years ago. We had a weeklong rental, an upstairs apartment in a frowsy old house that had been divided up to accommodate people just like us. It was grassy, though, and shady, with a nice stretch of road to walk, and we had discovered a small horse farm nearby, which became a popular destination for keeping the kids amused. We would stand by the roadside, pressed against the wooden fence, and watch the horses being exercised in the corral. Mara might have been ten or eleven that summer, Liam four or five, and I somewhere in my late forties. I do all this approximate figuring because my epiphany—I think it counts as one—had everything to do with ages and proportions.

It was the very end of a beautiful summer afternoon, the light beginning to slant. But though I was vacationing, I was also trying very hard to get some writing done, to bring a book project around to completion. It was because I wanted to think, to stew in my own notions, that I begged off when Lynn and the kids started down the road on another walk. I waved good-bye, I remember, and then sat myself down on a steep, grassy verge in front of the house and watched. They were moving slowly, one or both kids dawdling. I sat and stared at them, and as I did I felt come over me, gradually, the clearest and sweetest melancholy. It was as if I had suddenly moved out of myself, pulling away and rising like some insect that has left its transparent shell stuck to the branch of a tree. I was in my body, aware of everything around me, but I was above it at the same time. It was as if the needle on the balance had drawn up completely straight; the string I plucked was exactly in tune. I watched my wife and two kids walking away from me down the road and I got it. I was *exactly* in the middle—of the afternoon, of the summer, of an actuarial life, of the great generational cycle. Outlined against the horizon in front of me were those three shapes, and behind me, imagined on the opposite horizon, were my own two parents, both still alive and in good health, just coming into their seventies. I was in the middle, at once a son, a father, and something else: a man with plans and projects in his head, no one's person. It was the frailest and most temporary alignment, and the sensation just then of everything holding steady, hovering in place, exalted me, just as the knowledge that it had to change filled me with sorrow. I took a breath and swallowed my metaphysics. I headed in to use the bit of time I had to do my work. For if parenting held any practical lesson for me, it was that I had to learn to stake out time, to filch every little scrap I could.

Something's happened, just now, here, between one glance and the next. There were two sails in view beyond the line of the pier, but when I look I see only one. The blue sail. Caleb's. Fatherhood compresses into a single pulse, long enough for me to jump off the edge of the deck to the sand and start jogging around the ropes and old buoys to where the pier comes to shore, and when I reached that point I ducked and went under, to get to the other side where I could see. As I straightened up to look I saw there was just the one boat, and I couldn't get a clear picture of the rest. There were other boats, sailboats, bobbing at anchor, just masts. I scoured the water surface between—nothing. I was not afraid exactly, but definitely anxious. Liam could swim, he had a life vest, he was right there somewhere. And yes, yes, there—I centered in—I saw something moving right next to one of the anchored boats. A small commotion. Caleb's Sunfish looked to be heeling around in that direction. Liam had obviously tipped over; he was there fussing in the water next to his capsized boat.

I knew, sure as anything, that he would not be able to right the thing by himself. And Caleb wouldn't be able to do much. Still not worried, I also knew I should tell the girl at the rental shack so that she could get someone out to give him a hand.

When I got back, the girl was standing on her crate with binoculars. She was ahead of me. "I've got Jimmy on his way to check it out." I turned and saw a small launch chugging toward pier's end. "He'll just bring them in," she said. "It's getting kind of blowy out there." And so it was. I glanced up and saw that our blue day had gone completely cloudy and that the water was turning choppy. I went back to my chair to wait.

There is no guide to any of this. Kids get older in sudden jumps and with each jump the scramble begins. Strategies that worked so reliably one day are useless in the face of the new. Moods, secrecies, distances, brash eruptions. You know things are shifting when you suddenly find yourself choosing your words, reading cues like you never had to before. I had thought the family, our blustering foursome, immutable until Mara arrived at adolescence. Then she changed. She grew moody, and these moods were not something she could leave at home when vacation time came. This altered everything. It marked out before and after. *Before* was all of our innocent routines: walking to the beach, to the pond, or getting ice cream or lounging in front of a rented movie, cracking jokes. *After* was a new unknown that threw so much about family life into question. Who were we that this young person would find a thousand reasons not to be with us? Who was she to take us in with evaluating eyes; to wander off on self-errands that left the rest of us wanting? "Family" now felt like something picked apart. Where was our invincibility?

To be a parent, a father, was suddenly to contend with the world washing in. Or adulthood. Adulthood is a force that breaks against the easy containment of childhood. Fatherhood has its first incarnation as a presiding and protecting. Later it becomes a kind of brokering. We start to run interference between the world as we know it and the world as our children are learning about it. If early parenting is about the fostering of innocence, and the upholding of certain illusions—to give the self time to build itself—the later stage of parenting asks for a growing recognition of sorrow, cruelty, greed, of the whole unadorned truth of things. The truth that the child, now adolescent, will encounter, but marked and annotated and put into perspective.

The last few of our Cape summers have made me feel this acutely, more than our daily-world interactions. The idea of vacation is so imbued with heedlessness and innocence—the stock imagery of families relaxing together—that any small sadness or disaffection is amplified. The kitschy menu board at the clam shack seems to mock us, the shopwindow posters, as do the happy blond groups bicycling along the beach road. For there is our teenager moping in the backseat, on her towel, lying curled up in bed as if nothing in the world is worth the exertion of sitting up. At times the daily business left behind can seem like the real vacation, the place to get back to.

I'm on my feet again. Foreground and background—my thought and my immediate awareness—seem to merge as soon as I see the procession come into view from behind the pier. The launch with two silhouettes—one of them Liam's. And then, behind, the Sunfish with sail down, on a tow, Caleb's blue-sailed boat trails behind. All's well, I think, shaking my head. The girl from the rental desk makes her way down to the beach. I wave to Liam, wait for some nod. But though he seems to take me in I get no response. He is sitting up very straight in the back of the launch, looking the way prisoners always do in movies.

I jump down from the deck and join the girl on the beach. Jimmy has unhooked the Sunfish and pushed it toward shore; he turns the boat to dock it at the pier. Liam remains upright in his seat. He doesn't respond when Caleb passes the launch on his way in.

A few minutes later, I watch him coming toward me along the pier, his life vest still buckled tight. He looks pale, and when he draws closer and I reach to touch his shoulder, I catch something new in his expression. He's afraid.

The story comes out in jags, and not right away. First we all have to gather together again. Lynn arrives from her errands around town and we mill around for a few minutes collecting our things. And then the four of us are back on the main street, scouting for a restaurant where we can sit. Only when we get a table and sit does Liam open up. It jars me. He switches into an edgy sort of agitation, not like him, talking fast and using his hands. I'm expecting some dramatic bluster, but I'm wrong. "I thought I was going to drown," he says. The voice itself, the tone, is flat. I know he's serious. "I was in irons—facing right into the wind—and then I got pushed into this other boat." We're at our table on the enclosed patio of a big bayside restaurant, paying full attention. In the five minutes since we arrived the sky has gone black—the wind is shaking the plastic around us, the first drops come trailing down.

The whole story comes out once we've placed our order. And now I start to put it together, the way he sat in the boat, the look on his face when he came toward me. I get the surface of it, then I get more. And now as I write I'm feeling still other layers. I feel the shadow of the wing—the dread—as I did when he was talking. Liam could have drowned, it could have happened. He will need to tell it again and again to us before that look on his face goes away.

He was doing fine, he claimed, until he passed the pier and found himself headed toward the moored boats. "I started to get scared," he says. The boats were coming up fast, and he tried to turn. "I messed up." I stare at his hands, big and red. "I got turned around and all of a sudden I was in irons." I can see he likes the phrase. "My boat got pushed back into this other boat and then my tiller got caught in its rope." He pauses to get the sequence straight, and takes a breath. I think how I'd seen none of this, only the triangular peak of his red sail stalled in the distance. He explains how he was trying to work the tiller free with one hand while using his other to jostle the boom back and forth in hopes of catching some wind. And then—

"I don't really know what happened, something screwed up. I got the tiller free, but the boom whipped around and all of a sudden it pulled the rope around my neck." That was when it happened. His boat had heeled over with a rush, jerking him into the water—with the rope suddenly around his neck. The force of capsizing instantly tightened the noose and as the mast was pulled down to the water he could barely get his hand in between the rope and his throat. He was being pulled down by the boat. He panicked. He thought he was drowning. And then somehow, he doesn't know how, he slipped his head free.

He told his tale a number of times that night, getting his version the way he wanted it, gradually putting the picture outside himself, giving it over to us. As we listened, we all did that primitive thing. We kept reaching over to touch him. I put my hand on his, Lynn leaned her head against him, Caleb tapped his shoulder. The three of us were making him real again, planting him in our midst, taking him back from that "almost."

"You could have drowned, my God—" We said it again and again as the rain hammered down. And we talked about it for the rest of the night. We hovered around, bringing the "almost" in close and then fending it off again. I thought of myself there on the deck, oblivious, and could not resist extrapolating: a big obvious message about how it is between parents and their children—between any people who are close, really—how it snarls up together, all the vigilance and ignorance, luck and readiness, love and fear. We know nothing.

Four days before we have to leave the Truro house, Mara arrives. We are the basic unit at last—Caleb took the ferry back to Boston the day after the sailing episode. It feels strange, sweet. But the ground feeling, the joy, of having everyone together in the same place, with nothing on the schedule except trips to the ocean and the making of meals, is overlaid with darker tones. Mara is still in her mood, it's obvious. She tells us that she has been having bad dreams and feeling anxious every night. I see her on the couch, reading a magazine, looking for all the world like a young woman relaxing with her family, except that something in the shoulders, the tilt of the head, gives her away.

Mara gets through the first night easily enough. In fact, she sleeps like she hasn't slept in a long time, dead-weight sleep. Sleep like I have not had for decades. She had told me to wake her early, that she would join me for my walk, and once I've had my coffee I try. But after a few separate prods I give it up. I go alone, all the way down the long hill to the deli-market to buy the papers. Heading back, I think about our long season of morning walks. It lasted for years, that season, and I remember it often. How we moved in companionable solitudes, rarely breaking into talk. We walked almost every day, miles at a time. She told me once, later, that she did it to keep me from being sad. I may have been doing it for the same reason—we were tunneling the mountain from opposite sides. But then our morning schedules changed and we tapered off.

I open the sliding door off the deck quietly—everyone is still sleeping—and I drop the *Times* and *Globe* on the kitchen counter. I see Mara sprawled on her bed much as I left her. I pause in the doorway and study her. I forget in which Greek myth one of the gods drapes a cloth woven from gold over a sleeper's body, but I think of that as I stand there. I see how her face goes all the way back to first innocence.

Mara does seem happier now. Being away, or being with us, has given her a lift. She starts to crack wise, which is always a sign. And she is eager to go shopping with Lynn in Provincetown. That next day they disappear for a few hours. And then in the late afternoon we all go to the beach. The tide is low, the light spectacular. Lynn and Liam take their boogie boards and head down to where the waves are breaking. Mara wraps herself in a towel and reads Nabokov's *Ada*. I just stare, first to the left where the beach gradually merges into dune line, then, with a visceral pleasure—*There is nothing like this,* I think—over to the right, where the flat sand reaches into the faintest mist and the shoreline at every second takes that quick-silver print of water, where I see the silhouettes of people standing and wading and swimming in the distance.

Mara doesn't go in. There was a time when she would just *fling* herself into the tallest waves she could find. She would yowl and shake herself and do it again. I feel like something about all this water, though, is beginning to reach up to her now, as if she might be almost ready to push up off her towel and march down. But not yet. We sit side by side and watch Liam, our appointed stone gatherer. Lynn had asked him to find some large ocean stones for her garden. Liam likes this kind of thing, a task. He has his big goggles on and every few seconds we see him go arsy-turvy into the waves, and then up he comes, arm lifted high, clutching the next prize, which he stops to inspect for a moment and then either hurls to the shore or releases back into the water. The Sunfish episode has receded. This is in keeping with his style. If life backs up and grows scary for Mara, for Liam it catches, pauses, and then rushes on again. They are so very differ-ent, and I look from one to the other as if recognizing that essential fact. It's the kind of thing I might say to Lynn, but she's not here. She's out swimming—I see her paralleling the shore, a small moving shape down to my left. I would tell Mara, but Mara is all at once up. While we were both sitting there watching Liam the moment came. She has dropped her towel and is on her feet. With a quick over-the-shoulder glance she tromps down the sand and right to the water's edge. No running back and forth to work up to action. She pushes her hair back behind her ears and steps thigh-deep into the water. A flinch—I feel the sympathetic shock—and then she's in, under, three seconds vanished, and up with a thrust. And in again. I want to shout something, but I don't. I wish for the cold salt to scour her clean.

Liam, I see, has noticed his sister in the water. This makes him happy. I can tell. He turns away from the rock project and goes dolphin-bounding toward her. He loves company, and the company of his sister especially. When she can be gotten to. He wants to cruise the waves with her now, standing by her side. Nothing in common between their body types—he dwarfs her. But they are brother and sister, something in the way they stand side by side tells on them. They share humor—it's invisible, but I recognize it—and care. They share a certain brashness, too. When the big wave they've been waiting for arrives they push into it with the same slugging lunge. Two heads, and then, right when the wave thins to breaking, two tumbling oblongs flashing against the green.

Walden

This morning I got myself into Walden Pond again, the third time this summer, which is nothing at all when I remember certain summers before, but for all sorts of reasons it felt like a victory, another step taken on what I like to think is a road back to something. This sounds more dramatic than I mean it to. But I have been having a long and complicated struggle in my heart and I know that the swimming is part of it. I don't just mean pulling myself forward through water, but everything that surrounds the act: the getting ready, the looking and thinking and nonthinking, the last deep breath and the dive, and all the things that happen then, compressed for me in the image of the first bubbles streaming off my extended fingers. I'm talking about being in lakes and ponds now, though if I go on about the subject, I'll have to talk about pools, all the dozens of pools, and coaches, and camps, and my whole teenage frenzy of wanting to be a team swimmer. Maybe this is why I've never really written about it before: I find just too many layers bound up with too many different things. It goes so far back. Long before there were pools and meets, there were the years at Walnut Lake, starting with the earliest times of growing up and then, later, the period when my father thought he would train me and turn me into a competitor. All these phases are still somehow with me every time I take that first time-obliterating plunge.

To fix on this timeless feeling is paradoxical, I realize, given how much of my swimming was for years about the opposite, about clock time: getting through whatever distance as quickly as possible. But this is not the swimming that matters anymore, though the memories of that are still there with every stroke; what matters is the other, the lake and pond swimming, where I can plunge in and feel my whole existence peeling away from me. I felt it again just this morning: I set my glasses aside, waded a few feet into the shallows, and then dove. All time, no time, everything just silvery bright bubbles and light and skin sensation, and each stroke I took after I reached the surface again was just a coda to that.

But if this is all so perfect, so precious, then why all the gaps between—and the great reluctance? Why so long before I decided to come to Walden again? My refusals go to the core of my life, and I don't know that I fully understand them. I have my guesses—that my being away has been all about my sense of what I do and don't deserve, about how much I believe that my life is still mine to make, is still open to me. Metaphysical sounding, yes, but for me swimming is like that.

I don't remember my earliest times, have no clear picture of my original baptism—not the way I can remember finding the line of balance on a bike, say, where it felt like my whole relation to space was suddenly pulled up right. I know that my parents sometimes took my sister, Andra, and me to the free-form cement pools at Cranbrook when we were both little. They were called Baby Jonah and Big Jonah, and on the observation balcony up at street level there was a Carl Milles fountain of Jonah balanced on the whale and spewing water from his mouth. My mother has photos of the two of us at both, a few of these from that short-lived era of yellow-coloration exposure. In one, I'm standing on the grass right next to the wide, smooth concrete lip of Big Jonah, a pool I would not have been ready for then. I am wispy thin and wear a tiny little suit that barely covers my front. The strange color of the photo has over time created a memory of special happiness, as if that one moment had a secret lemony warmth of its own.

The distance between the man now at the desk and the boy on the grassy verge is immense when calculated in land miles, but not much at all in water measure. There he stands, not three feet from the element, and here I was, fully immersed, just a few hours ago. And one of the surprises of water, of thinking underwater, thinking with breath held and the whole body sweeping along the coolness, is that things shift. Feelings and wants for some reason pull in very close, and daylight plans and projects move away almost beyond call.

I dove in this morning and automatically did what I have done since I was a boy: I scooped back my extended arms and oared myself quickly forward, frog-kicking and reaching forward again, feeling my hair go flat against my head, making the low underwater humming sound that comes so naturally when I am suddenly alone. I surfaced directly into a crawl stroke, which I pushed on with for a good ten breaths—four long strokes per breath—before pausing to see where I was. Nearsighted as I am—and this is a whole other part of swimming for me—I could take only the most obvious bearings. I pointed myself toward a wooded jut on the left side of the pond, maybe halfway along the shore. I made it my destination. My plan was to swim to the jut and turn around. As recently as two summers ago that would have been just the first leg. But I'm not counting that way now, not much. I'm happy enough to think I'll get to the point and back. Not that I couldn't do a good deal more than that if I wanted, but like I said, things have changed.

The great era of childhood swimming started when we moved to the house on Tahquamenon when I was in the first grade. We had beach rights to Walnut Lake, which was a few minutes away, and whole summers were taken up by the same basic routine, which was that my mother would drive Andra and me down to the beach in the late morning, and the three of us would set out our towels side by side on the sand, and then I would run as fast as I could to the end of the long dock, where I abruptly stopped and drew myself up straight. I waited to feel the world catch up with me and then slowly nerved up to dive. I would stand for a long time, looking down, imagining the first impact. This has always been how I do it. Even today I put myself through the same long pause, the negotiation, making myself ready for the change of state.

Those first years at the lake I mainly played and dove. The swimming area was sandy near the shore and then fell off quite suddenly into darker, deeper water and weeds. I loved the place where the drop began. I always had a sense of crossing into mystery, paddling and looking down to see the tops of the wavery weed stalks far below. And of course the water would get immediately cooler there, a coolness I could reach into by taking a breath and pulling myself down and down. Somewhere along the way I learned the basic strokes and even got fairly good at the crawl and backstroke. I could pass hours just pushing off from the barrels of the dock and churning my way into the swimming area, racing to one of the floating docks in the distance.

When I was older, nine or ten, I fell under the admiration spell of two brothers, our neighbors a few houses over, Don and Dave Robertson, who were both serious swimmers. Dave, the older brother, was a star on the high school team, and Don, who was two grades ahead of me, swam the most beautiful butterfly—fast and clean. Both were in some way protégés of the local high school coach, Corey Van Fleet, and at that point Don may have already started working at Corey's summer swimming camp. I don't remember this clearly, though I know that when I finally went to Camp Corwood a few summers later, he was already an established counselor. Before all that, though, he was just a lanky, flat-bodied, blond-haired kid with an amazing stroke, and from whenever it was that I first saw him cutting through the water between the docks, doing his butterfly or his effortless-looking crawl, I wanted to be a real swimmer, just like him. The feeling was immediate and intense, and it took no account of the difference between us—the fact that Don was strong and lean and built for it, while I was not at all athletic. Still, swimming became my dream, and those summers at the end of grade school and through junior high I spent all my free time in the water, swimming back and forth between the docks, counting time in my head as if I were racing a clock, practicing my crawl, my backstroke.

At some point early on in my obsession my father got involved with my practicing. This was unusual. He lived mostly for his architecture and was not one for father-son activities, but with this one interest something sparked for him. He had been a swimmer back in Latvia—you could still see it in his smooth easy stroke—and he was a great believer in training. He talked to me seriously. What I needed, he said, was discipline, and if I wanted, he would help me. I nodded. I wanted to be a swimmer. And with that began our season of early mornings. My father would come downstairs and touch me on the shoulder in the first light and I would quickly pull on my Speedo, find my towel, and go to the car. The world was so quiet at that hour. Pulling into the parking lot at the lake, we could see the mist hanging thick over the water. Morning after morning, my father stood on the end of the dock while I swam laps. He timed me with a stopwatch, calling out the numbers whenever I touched one dock or the other, and signaling things about my stroke, my kick, my breathing. He would use the same few gestures—I blinked to see him there in the distance—like crabbing up his hand to remind me to extend, not to chop. When we stopped, the air would still be cold, my suit dripping down my legs as I folded the towel in half and set it on the car seat.

The years of competition flow together now, though in fact there were epochs: first the junior high team coached by the mild-mannered Mr. Rosenthal, and then my two summers at Camp Corwood. I went because Corey was a legend, coach to the local champions, and I was desperate to get on the high school team. There for six weeks I lived in a cabin with other swimmers my age, all of us going through the same sunup to sundown schedule of running, lap swimming, and still more lap swimming with a few summer camp activities sandwiched in. The days were a torture at first—I had never worked out like that before. At first it felt endless, and I didn't know how I would make it. But day by day the repetitions pushed away everything else, until finally there was just the lake with its huge lane-markered area, and all of us launching off with every next whistle, racing each other, racing ourselves, finally just trying to hold on. By the end of that first camp summer I had become a believer.

I did make the high school team—as a backstroker. Camp Corwood had raised me to that level, but only just. I stayed on for a season before it came clear that I would never advance beyond a third-string backstroker—part of the bench. Being on the team meant punishing daily workouts, and being on the bench had me asking why I was doing it. I was just not built to be a swimmer. Still, I was more "fit" than I would ever be again. The hundred-meter repetitions, done every morning and afternoon out in the lake, had finally broken me through what Coach Corey called the "pain threshold." He said over and over again that no one could be a racer who hadn't gotten to the other side. On the other side you felt pain but you ignored it. I didn't know what he meant until it happened. Midworkout one day, I reached an exhaustion that felt absolute—I had used everything I had. But Corey wouldn't let me stop. Spotting me, zeroing in on my moment of doubt, he screamed, "Move it!" I can still picture this short, crew-cut man in his tank suit and white T-shirt in his place on the dock. The others had already started. I saw he was pointing at me. Jolted by pride and fear, I started again. There was no pushing off in deep water—you just lowered your head and started kicking and pulling. I was almost crying. I was sure I was done, empty. But then, stroke by stroke—it was like a scene in a movie—I felt myself rising up and out of it. It was as if I were taking a step back from myself; something changed in me. For a time I had a view of the path. I saw my chance. Alas, it was not enough, and as that long high school swim season wore on I felt my obsession drain away.

I wonder now: During that whole long era of teams and practices did I also keep this other feeling—of freedom, of my life dissolving? Or was I all business? I honestly can't remember. But I do know that many years then passed that had very little to do with water. When I quit team-swimming, I stopped altogether—no lakes or pools. My whole life had shifted. Where would I have gone to swim? In college I don't think I used the university pool more than a few times—once when I was so wired on Dexedrine from a late-semester all-nighter that I was afraid my heart was going to stop and I didn't dare try any laps. For those four years I got myself around on dry land with the rest of my long-haired tribe. Walnut Lake? I was only going home on visits then, and somehow those didn't include going to the lake. I had grown up and swimming was not what I did. And then, after college, I moved to Maine to start my life as a writer—that was how I thought of it. I lived with my girlfriend in a small apartment right on the ocean—but that was cold saltwater and only for hurtling plunges on the hottest summer afternoons.

These gaps are odd to contemplate, for this morning, steadily pushing toward that blurry jut of trees in the blurry distance, I felt an essential seamlessness—that this water has always been here, and I have always been moving through it. All my intervals vanished in the motion. And what a sweet erasing it was—to stop swimming for a moment and turn myself onto my back, see the sky suddenly absolute all around, and then, turning over, to give a quick little dolphin kick and a solid two-armed pull to propel myself into the coolness that is always right there—the coolness and the shadowy stillness where the bottom is invisible and there are only grades of deepening green.

When I was in my late twenties and living in Cambridge, I joined the local YMCA so that I could work out. I don't know that I was making an effort to reconnect with swimming so much as I was being determined to get exercise, and swimming and walking were what I knew best. When the weather was kind, I walked. The rest of the time I swam. It was a period of concerted discipline, I know, but all that comes back to me now is the grim smell and sensation of chlorine—in the eyes (despite goggles), on the skin, matted into the hair. I did my laps, my mile, for some months. And then—again, whole years dissolve on the screen—I became a full-fledged adult, a husband and father, a man with a work life that I could not have imagined during the interminable idling of my twenties. I was teaching and writing. I owned a house and was completely immersed in family life. What happened? I moved away from water and time surrounded me.

One aspect of this family life was that we tried to think of things that the three, then four, of us could all do. Going to Walden—a fifteen-minute drive from our house—became a staple activity for hot summer days, and though I'd been to the pond before, telling myself each visit that this was *Walden,* famous Walden, now it became another kind of revelation. I went with my wife and children in the afternoons, but—the real joy—I also went by myself in the early mornings. Here was a new ritual, a rejuvenation. I would rouse myself early almost every day in the summer. I took the back roads in the first light; I parked in a special place on the shoulder. Except for one or two regulars—we would nod from a distance—the pond was deserted. There was a calm that felt ancient, the water holding light in the center and dark-shadowed all along the shoreline, but I made no ceremony.

I set my towel on a rock, peeled off my T-shirt, and waded in, adjusting my goggles as I did. One deep steadying breath and then I dove.

The dive is the transformation. It never fails. The instant I immerse I am back, awake again inside that old illusion of a perfect timeless freedom. It's momentary—I know this—but it's also somehow deeper and more lasting than those few mere seconds under the surface. I am completely stretched out, weightless, flying forward, and in the cool I feel my whole outer self shearing away like a husk. The swimming itself, though it is its own delight, can't come up to that first exhilaration. For as soon as I start toward whatever destination I have set myself a ghost of the old discipline returns, I can't help it. I am full of sensation, free from my other life, but I am also focused; I find myself counting my strokes, four to a breath, ten breaths before I pause to repoint, swimming breaststroke.

I had years of this private rite while the kids were young, driving to the pond in the early light, wading in, swimming, and I often had the thought, in the water, or after, wet hair and windows open, driving the back roads through Lincoln, that nothing more could be added to life—there was no extra room.

When I get near the point, the jut, I slow down. Swimming in toward shore, I start watching the water below, looking for where the sandy bottom comes shelving up. After stopping, I always stand in place for few minutes, shaking off my goggles, panning my gaze around the perimeter, savoring the echoing silence that is so sudden after all my churning water noise. These moments have their own familiar track. Staring out, gazing at the trees on the far shore and their perfect matching reflections, gathering in the stillness, it's hard not to come to the same thought morning after morning: that it was like this a hundred and two hundred years ago, that generations have come and gone even as the perfect summer morning stays closed around me.

I hold the thought until it wanes. And then I take another of those deep swimming breaths. The destination is the midpoint, and the return is always a falling off. It's one thing to be making my way forward, out, another to be covering the same stretch, swimming right over the exhausted bubbles of my old wake.

Why did I stop those old morning swims—and swims altogether? What happened? It's hard to get back the motives and promptings of another time. But really I think it was the first hard strike of middle age, and then, after, a particular sadness that started to infiltrate my thoughts. It came slowly, almost a kind of seepage, reaching me in a hundred subtle ways, my loss of interest in my swims being just one mark of change. I didn't stop everything right away, nothing so drastic. I was still waking in the first light and certain mornings still called me out. I kept up with my walks. But even these weren't like before. It got easier and easier to linger with the paper. I would work through the crossword, then catch myself staring out into the middle distance as if I were still trying to remember a word. Things changed. The swimming slipped away—I found I no longer wanted to organize myself and get into the car. I pushed away my images of the pond, that sense of baptism. I accepted the new way. It seemed right.

This was more than just a slow shift of habits. There was also a deeper transition, one that relates to many things, including the feeling that was always the core of swimming. For the truth is that along with all that symbolic purging I experienced when I dove into fresh water, I always had a profound feeling of going toward. I mean less that I was headed to whatever point I had marked out for myself. My progress had very much to do with my sense of living as a *going toward*. All along I had believed that my life was a project just getting under way, an undertaking in its early, still erasable and correctable, stages. I made it well into middle age with the young man's sense of "any day now it will start." It was there in me as I pushed strollers, wrote mortgage checks, and positioned myself in front of students in one classroom after another. I never thought of it this way. I only understood what it meant when it started to slip away. A life cliché, but so be it. This is what swimming—and then no longer swimming—in the pond is really about. It's about how in my midfifties I found myself moving through my days with the obscure sense that some elusive vital thing had been slowly siphoned out. There was no lightning bolt. Only very gradually did I connect this with my reluctance about heading out the door—to hike, to get into water. It was not that I no longer enjoyed those things for themselves. It was, I saw, that whenever I did walk or swim I would end up facing the fact that that old feeling of just getting started was gone, and that another feeling had taken its place.

Making my way back—to my towel, to the spot marked for me by the blurry pale shape of the beach house—I am a slower, more dutiful swimmer. I feel myself taking longer strokes, pacing out my energy. The water is still fine, and the sky is still blue and clear when I pause and flip onto my back, but now it's not open vista I'm swimming toward, but a particular spot to the right of the beach house, the place on the top step where I've left my folded towel and glasses and shorts. And I'm thinking different thoughts, I can't help it. I'm starting to focus on what I need to do, how I'll drive home and eat and collect my papers and get ready to drive into the city.

This other feeling, though—what is it? It's the opposite of getting started, I would say. It is, rather, the recognition that one has long since started, has done and done—carried out the long-repeated doing that makes a life—and that there will be with every year less on offer. This is not a profession of despair, nothing like that. I simply find myself facing the fact that the light has changed, that the atmosphere of wanting is not what it was in earlier days. How could it be? Alas, we can't help making our way forward by way of comparison. We so naturally view ourselves in terms of the desires that launched us on our private schemes, drew up our charts, and when those desires change, or wane, as they must, then our outlook has to shift. I think now that I stopped swimming for as long as I did because for me swimming had always been the active expression of that desire. To go into water was, strange as it sounds, to hypothesize my future. And when the larger sense of that future changed in me, I felt my desire go away. I would wake up so many mornings and test the idea in my mind: Could I see myself taking that first clean plunge? In my bitterness and sadness, I could not. Something I'd felt eager about for so long now felt like a chore. And this feeling continued in me.

And yet here I am—or was this morning—making my way out, and then back, and doing so, if not with an innocently glad heart, then at least without that terrible freight of resistance. What changed? Truthfully, I don't know, nothing I can readily point to. But somewhere in the heat and oppression of these summer days, not by act of choice but following some hidden tropism, whatever had first turned in me started to turn again—not undoing or reversing itself, not redeeming all sadness and loss, but showing me that the heart, or will, or whatever it is that holds the power of our self-making, can still deliver surprise. It was really just a few weeks ago that I woke and found myself ready for an early-morning Walden swim. A shift. I didn't even need to lie there and think it over. I could feel the quiet of the shore without being there, and could almost taste the sweet water on my lips. It felt like just the thing. I wanted that water, that new erasure.

The Walk

On most summer mornings, I come to when the last dark meets the first light and my friend the ur-bird starts up somewhere deep in the bushes out back, laying the ground for whatever will be my mind's first step. The sound is so familiar that I hardly take it in—part of a larger general stirring—but it touches off the first impulse: to be up and out, in it, walking.

Not right away, though. Not before slow strong coffee and a long time spent just staring. Staring is part of the coming to, though I wonder, writing this, "Coming to *what?*" as if there were a destination, some place of arrival. At this hour the gaze really is that, a gaze, hardly moving, but every shift is as momentous as turning a page in a philosophy book. I sit in the living room, convinced that I can track the gradual changing of the light—less by seeing the light itself than by noticing how the books on the shelves and the pictures on the walls, even the pencils and clips and the papers on the coffee table, seem to be emerging—almost, I would say, *verging,* though on what I couldn't say. The fact, in any case, hardly bothers our small black cat, who lies curled on the back of the couch and marks the indoor silence with his huffing little snore.

After a while I begin to feel it: the restlessness, snaking up my legs and through the rest of me, the urge to be out in that early air by myself, before anyone else gets the idea, long before the garage doors all through the neighborhood collectively rise for the cars, and suddenly, without in any way deciding it, I'm up, my empty cup on the kitchen counter, the screen door easing shut against my hand—as if even the lightest click might rouse my sleepers in their caves. With this comes the inevitable question: Which way? Which of my five or six routes should I take? Surely it makes no difference; surely the fate of the whole day and the life to come hangs in the balance. I loosely juggle my options to the end of the street, but then make an impetuous right, cutting my alternatives in half, flashing as

I do on my remaining choices: up Crescent Hill and down to the reservoir, or left into Reed's Brook Park.

But no, Reed's is too short a walk, too tight a noose. I'm willing to sacrifice the red-winged blackbirds in the marsh and our lone heron brooding in his perpetual blue study, because today I need to cover distance, get some accumulation, work up to things. Everything feels locked up, to the point where I catch myself zooming in with an obsessive fascination on the mechanical to-and-fro thrust of my legs, the apparition of my shoes against the concrete. I can almost feel the dreary formulas of physics working through my motions—coefficients and vectors, bone, muscle, surges of directed effort—until some gust of grace makes me lift my eyes from the street and into the thick of an enormous tree hung with green waxy leaves, and all my earnest focus blows right off.

This, right here, is the first real showing of the day, the one point when I'm able to take it in unmade, wide open, with everything still to be announced. I can feel my own rhythm start to lift me up and tune me to the swing of walking, that growing catch-pull connection between the body's exertion and whatever is passing through my head. I get a quick memory slice of text, Stephen Dedalus, the man with the world in his head, walking by the sea at Sandymount strand: *thought through my eyes,* he said—or thought—and I try to hold that (staring *is* thinking) as I come up to the corner where Summer Street meets Reed, a stretch of road that will be a flurry of cars in an hour. All those monomaniacal work-eagles still damp from their showers. But at this moment I see only the soft pink haze of the sun coming over the far eastern horizon. And I'm triggered, as I often am right here, to see myself captured in a kind of film loop, a montage of repetitions. I imagine a high-speed farrago of all my mornings of crossing at this spot, by now my *years* of mornings, and think how if I could actually *watch* such a film collage, I'd be all but wiped out by the parade of my self-approximations: the dull repeated repertoire of clothes and shoes, the slumping posture, slump, slump, always the same, and—worse—how if I pulled the lens in close I'd have to mark the steady wearing out of the face, the thing that always hits me first when I'm handed an old photo of myself. *Look at him!* I want to say. As if the gaze of the world should come to rest for one long beat, no more, on this face—not so much on the fact of it, but on the terrible indignity of the whole business, so we could all in aggrieved chorus cry out, *To what end is this happening?*

One flinch is enough: I'm already moving on, and just collecting myself for the first hill pushes the mutability meditation aside.

Walking—thinking by way of the body, the feet and legs, filtering the immediate world with senses on high—I'm so much more open to the whims of association than I am when I'm at my desk with my lineup of plans in front of me. I also feel it—though not always—as a movement toward writing, for at a certain point in my circuit, I can't say how this happens, a different kind of sifting of words begins. None of this is remotely orderly—just phrases breaking in on the subthreshold murmur. Breaking in and snagging but then so often repeating, for these words and phrases are quickly taken up into the body's rhythm. Uncensored idiocies mainly, bits coughed up from the bit hoard, childhood mantras, lines of poetry (usually misremembered), and some of these will even erupt out of the mind and into voice, so that I might be coming up over the hill, automatically turning my head for the first view of the reservoir down below, and at the same time be saying out loud something like "full fathom five" or "what's the use?" or "I'm *not* gonna pay a lot for this fucking muffler"—no profundity in any of it, not even when context is established, but at the same time part of something in the works.

What *is* in the works, by the slowest of slow stages, is a shifting out of the ambient sleep-tuned state and into whatever is taking over. The word-self. It happens in increments. One thought moves in, unannounced, linking to something I might have mumbled a minute before, but now adding on, fitting edges, so that by the time I'm down the short steep hill, slipping into the reservoir through the opening in the fence, I really am gaining on the day's mind. I feel those phrases linking into larger units of coherence, even as I also want to stall the process off. But there's no real stopping it, finally. Only a hope of tugging on the reins a bit, urging these first inklings in the right direction, to let them be something more than landing sites for my endless opportunistic anxieties.

The day becomes a presence now, looming up over the empty soccer field and down over the reservoir, already exerting a pull of its own, an undertow—an energy very likely unrelated to anything I intend or imagine. Which explains something more about the walk—that it's not just an elaborate wake-up dance, it's also my way of gathering evidence, reading the whole chart of atmospheric signs so that I can try to put the self in accord. Much is decided by what associations come, what memories are sparked, how I parry the ongoing shuffle of particulars. A squirrel barking at me from a nearby branch sends me one way, an abandoned bag full of empties right here on the ground another. I'm skirting the left side of the water now, walking over the bridge that spans the water lock, with its clunky, slightly impressive gear works—our vaunted civic engineering. At the same time, behind a fence and through a thin screen of trees, I face the unavoidable boxy bland units of public housing. Everything registers. And between the press of civic and public it's hard to resist the suck of the ordinary on the mind. Where is the wildness? What happened to danger, the risk, the thrill of living? I ask these things automatically. But on certain days, most days, when I can't bear to face this rendition of who I am—the homeowner, taxpayer, voting citizen—I also move preemptively. I look up from the pebble path and throw my gaze forward, out over the tooth-marked bites of shore, into the distance.

Which is where I always see the swans. There's a whole family of them, maybe several. Singly, in pairs, they patrol the far reaches of the reservoir, the wilder part where the path turns to dirt pack and where the birches rear up. The white of these birds is always a surprise—and their calm is an instant corrective to whatever has begun to ail me. I can't look out at them there and not go right to Yeats. Swans, Yeats—but how much do we care for originality when we're alone? It's the Coole Park poem I'm remembering: *They paddle in the cold / Companionable streams or climb the air,* though I wonder if I have the words right. Never mind. The thing about poetry is that it's renewable—you can always linger with a good line.

Today I feel the liftoff of *or climb the air*—or CLIMB the AIR—and by God if it doesn't instigate that old swirl, more emotion than thought, stirring together Yeats and art and life—*life,* I mean—and obviously some deeper circuit has started sparking here because before I've even reached the last bend I get a slurring of fast sensations, and then it comes all at once, I'm hit straight on with it: a genuine pang full of the agitation of being young, young and still on the front side of life—blurring together my children, my students, a generalized memory of my own early times, all of us back then, how we would always be sitting around talking in those sideline places we found—I can picture us under trees, by lakes—so full of our untempered bravado, *we will never, we will always*—and all this nostalgia comes in one strong gust, which is maybe why it feels so raw and sweet, as if it's not to be mocked or even looked at fondly.

But I keep walking, and then this feeling too shifts away, ebbs, as I come through the last bend in the path; and now, in no way having coordinated it, I get off that track and push through the final brambly patch of woods. Then I take a breath and chug up the embankment to get to the street, suddenly back in the world, balancing on the raised concrete strip there, those last wispy thoughts vaporizing as I refocus, keeping myself way over on the shoulder to avoid what is now a steady stream of cars. Two or three good strides make absolute the shift from Yeats and fate and youth to the prose of breakfast and wake-up schedules for my sleepers. In fact, for the first time this morning I look at my watch (for the gesture of it) and it is here, finally, a quarter mile from my door, that I can get hold of the workday coming up. Not the part that has to do with writing—that has to stay a superstition, a possibility hidden inside the amorphous folds of whatever develops—but all the other business in front of me. The sequences. I see the commute, feel it clearly, the slow brake-and-pedal drag past Alewife Station and out Fresh Pond Parkway to Storrow Drive, where traffic finally breaks, and then I remember—I picture—like a reward, the cool basement office, still quiet, getting more and more real as I bump the lens slowly to take in the desk, my anchorage, the piles of envelopes exactly where I left them yesterday, the cup of blunt pencils and erratic pens, all the little to-do notes I've left on stray sheets of paper . . .

The author would like to thank Lynn Focht-Birkerts, Askold Melnyczuk, Tom Sleigh, Christopher Benfey, Tom Frick, Brad Morrow, Brigid Hughes, Rosamond Purcell, Wendy Lesser, Bill Pierce, Jane Dobija, Dinah Lenney, Ben George, Marc Smirnoff, Barrie Jean Borich, and Vivek Narayanan.

Sven **Birkerts** has been the editor of *AGNI* since July 2002. He is the author of eight books: *An Artificial Wilderness: Essays on Twentieth-Century Literature* (William Morrow), *The Electric Life: Essays on Modern Poetry* (William Morrow), *American Energies: Essays on Fiction* (William Morrow), *The Gutenberg Elegies: The Fate of Reading in an Electronic Age* (Faber & Faber), *Readings* (Graywolf), *My Sky Blue Trades: Growing Up Counter in a Contrary Time* (Viking), *Reading Life: Books for the Ages* (Graywolf), and *The Art of Time in Memoir: Then, Again* (Graywolf). He has edited *Tolstoy's Dictaphone: Technology and the Muse* (Graywolf), as well as *Writing Well* (with Donald Hall; Longman) and *Literature: The Evolving Canon* (Allyn & Bacon).

Birkerts has received grants from the Lila Wallace–Reader's Digest Foundation and the Guggenheim Foundation. He was winner of the Citation for Excellence in Reviewing from the National Book Critics Circle in 1985 and the Spielvogel-Diamonstein Award from PEN for the best book of essays in 1990. Birkerts has reviewed regularly for the *New York Times Book Review*, the *New Republic*, *Esquire*, the *Washington Post*, the *Atlantic*, *Mirabella*, *Parnassus*, the *Yale Review*, and other publications. He has taught writing at Harvard University, Emerson College, Amherst College, and Mount Holyoke College, and is the director of the graduate Bennington Writing Seminars. He lives in Arlington, Massachusetts, with his wife and two children.

Book design by Ann Sudmeier. Composition by BookMobile Design and Publishing Services, Minneapolis, Minnesota. Manufactured by Friesens on acid-free 100 percent postconsumer wastepaper.